Thank you...

... for purchasing this copy of Wet Play Today for ages 5-7. We hope you find it useful on those wet days when the children need occupying inside at break and playtimes.

Please note that photocopies can only be made for use by the purchasing institution. Supplying copies to other schools, institutions or individuals breaches the copyright licence. Thank you for your help in this.

This Wet Play Today book is part of our growing range of educational titles. Most of our books are individual workbooks but, due to popular demand, we are now introducing a greater number of photocopiable titles especially for teachers. You may like to look out for:

WET PLAY TODAY for ages 5-7, 7-9, 9-11

READING FOR LITERACY for Reception
                                and for ages 5-7, 7-8, 8-9, 9-10, 10-11

WRITING FOR LITERACY for ages 5-7, 7-8, 8-9, 9-10, 10-11

SPELLING FOR LITERACY for ages 5-7, 7-8, 8-9, 9-10, 10-11

NUMERACY TODAY for ages 5-7, 7-9, 9-11

HOMEWORK TODAY for ages 5-7, 7-8, 8-9, 9-10, 10-11

BEST HANDWRITING for ages 4-7, 7-11

To find details of our other publications, please visit our website: **www.acblack.com**

Contents

Contents

Join the Dots (1)

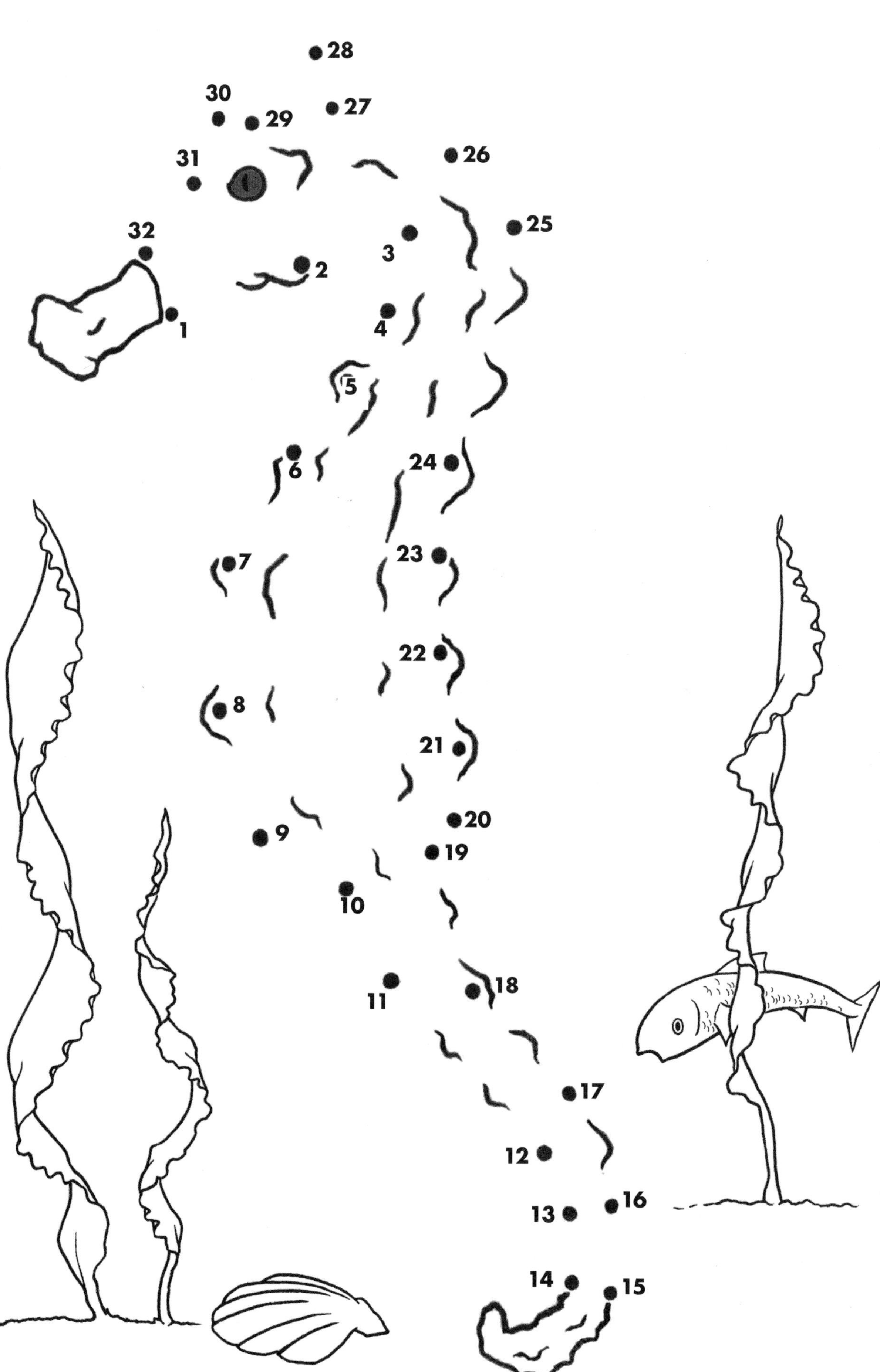

WET PLAY TODAY

Find the Shoes

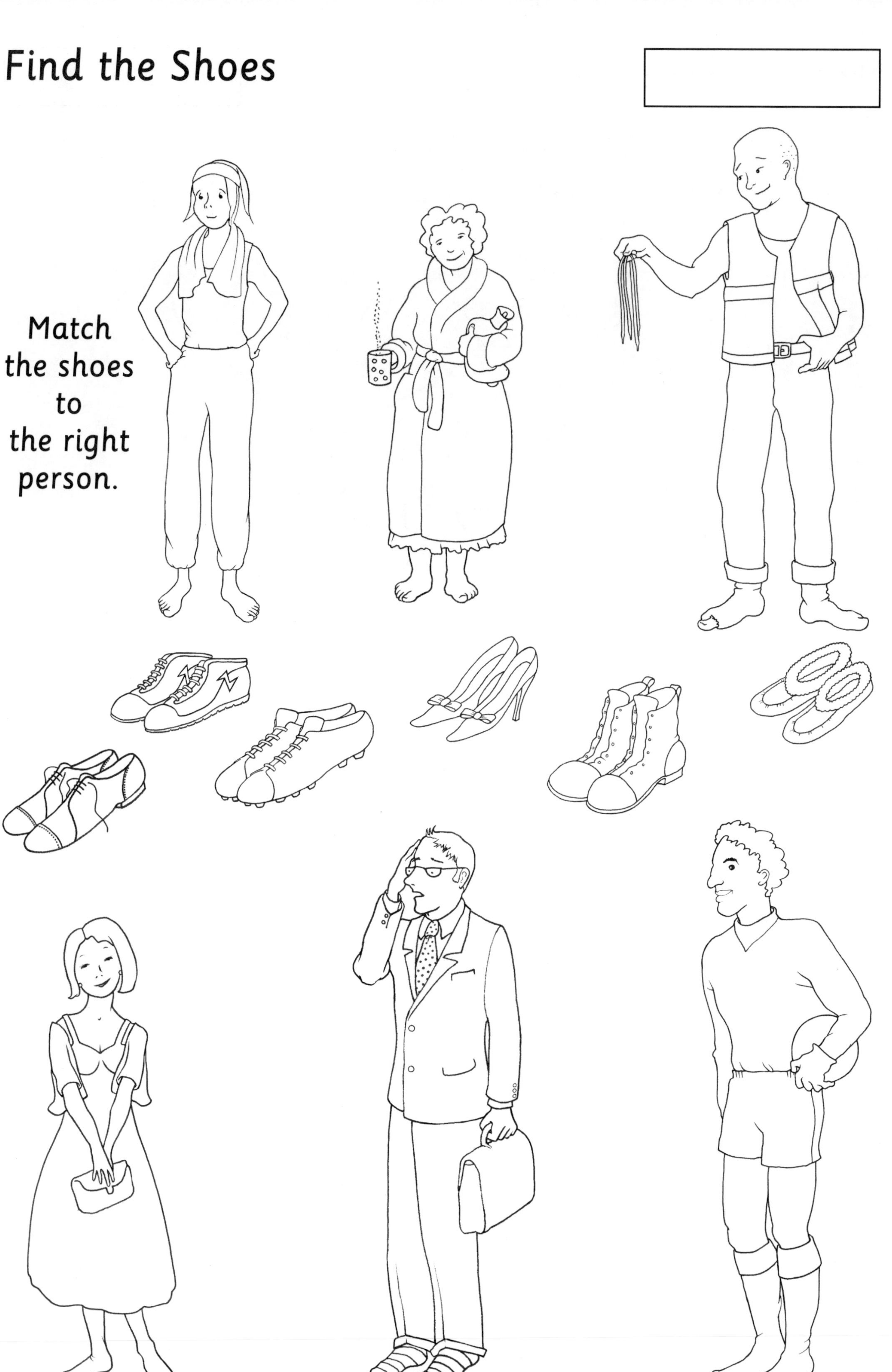

Match
the shoes
to
the right
person.

Can you find the 16 ice-creams hidden in the picture?

WET PLAY TODAY

Elephants

Can you spot the 10 differences between these two pictures?

Footballers

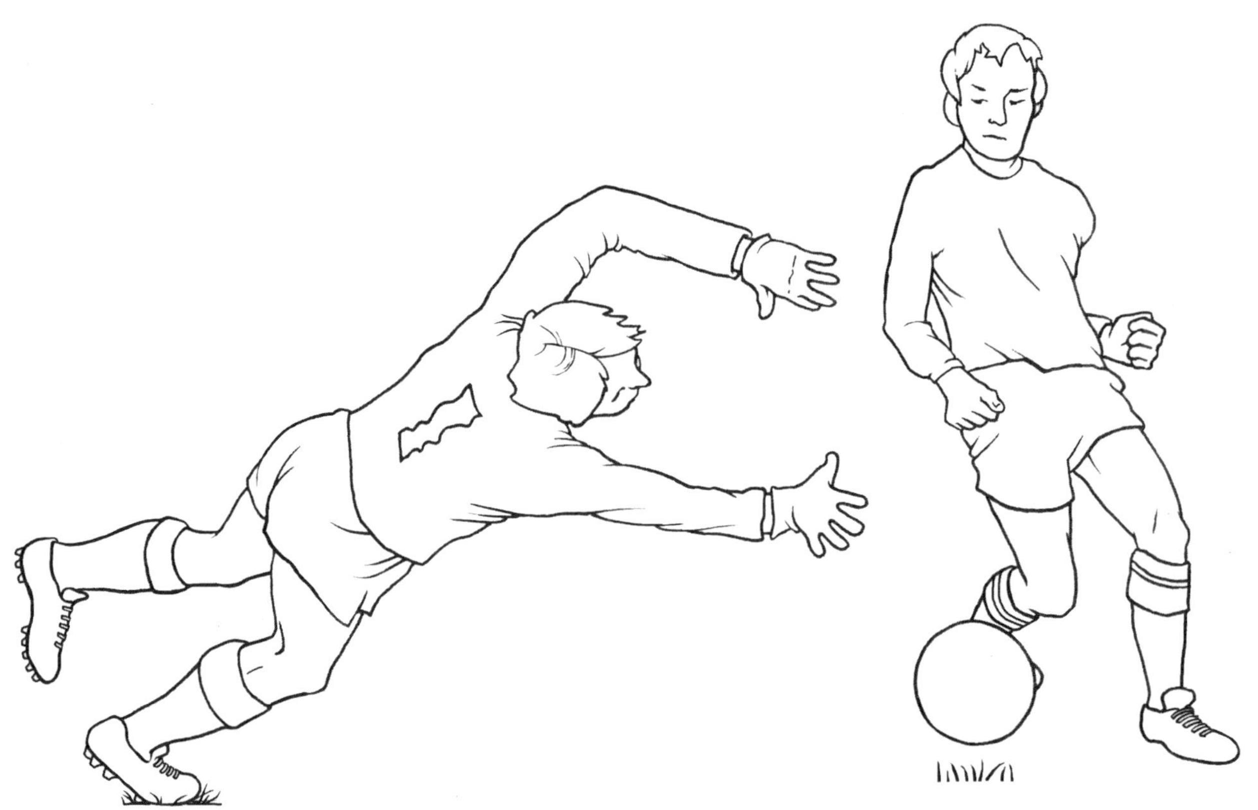

Can you spot the 10 differences between these two pictures?

Join the Dots (2)

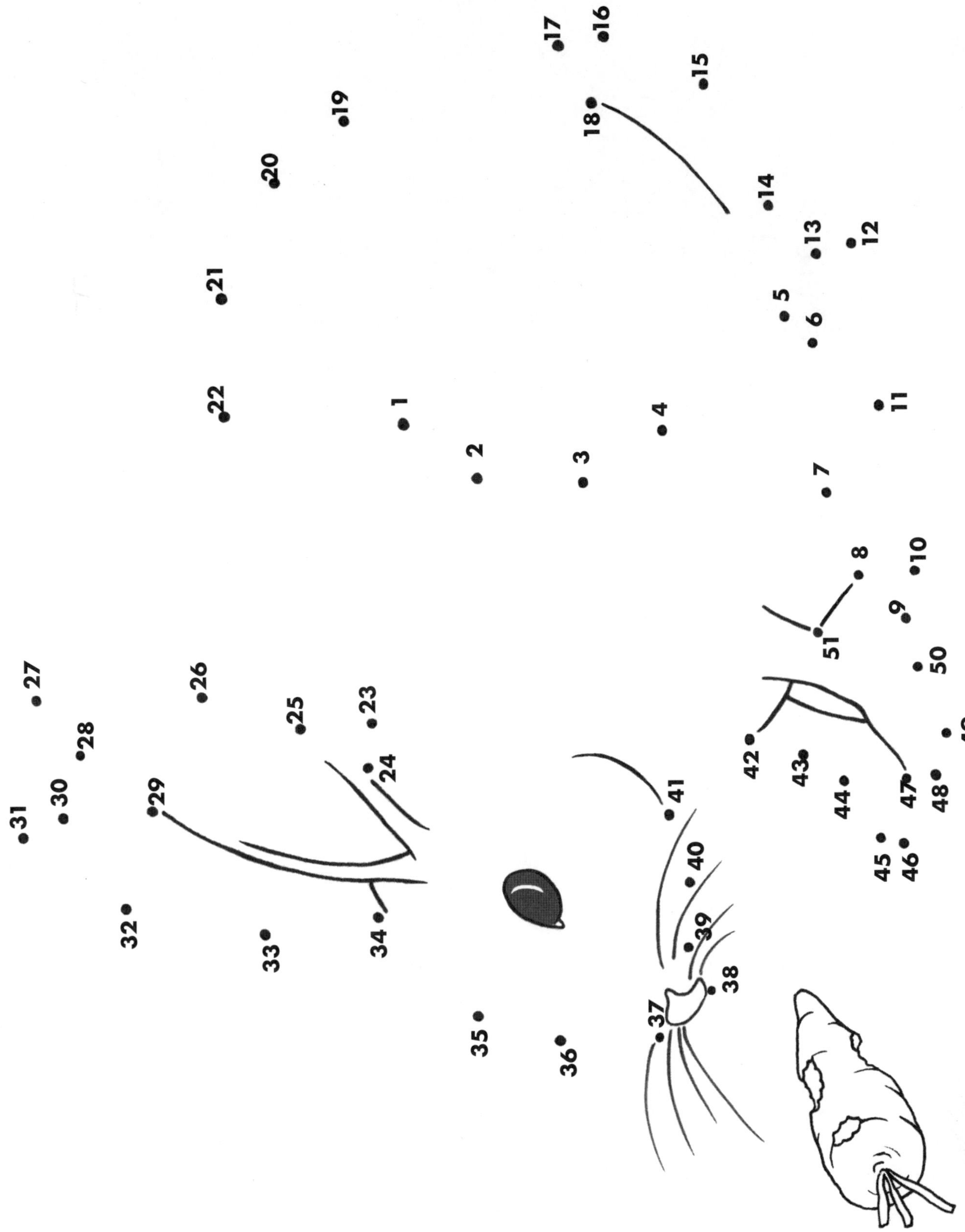

Join the Dots (3)

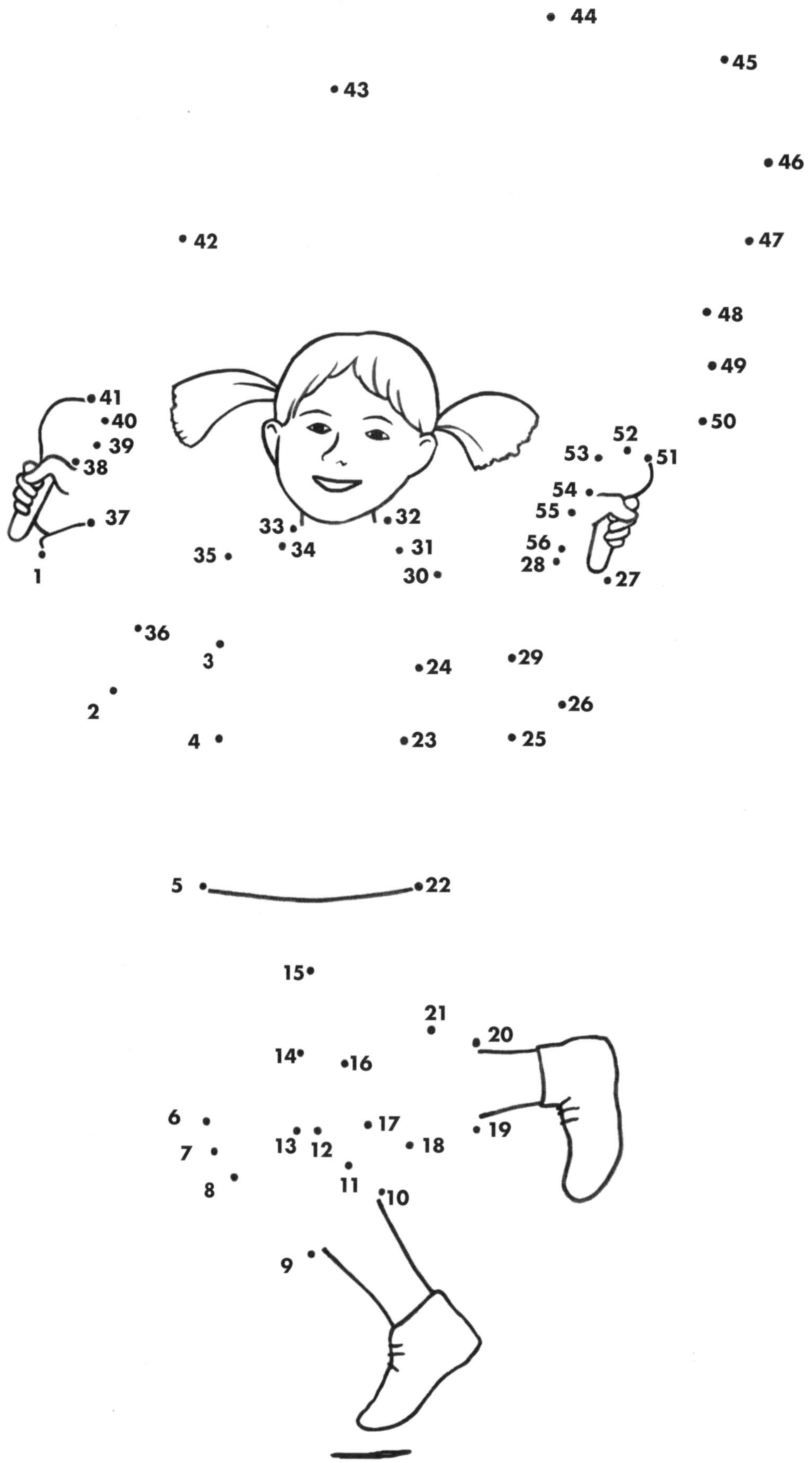

Colour the picture when you have finished.

Join the Dots (4)

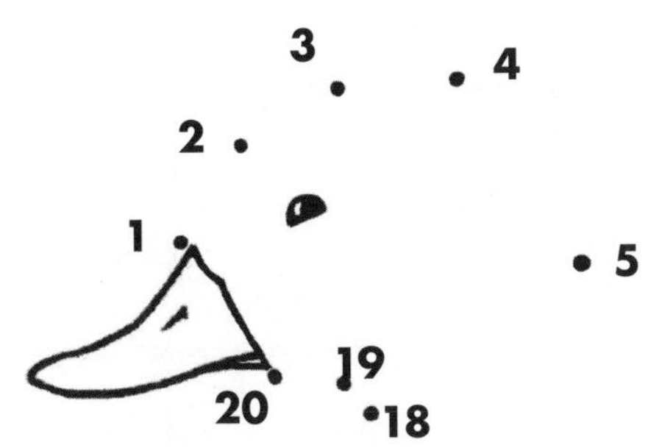

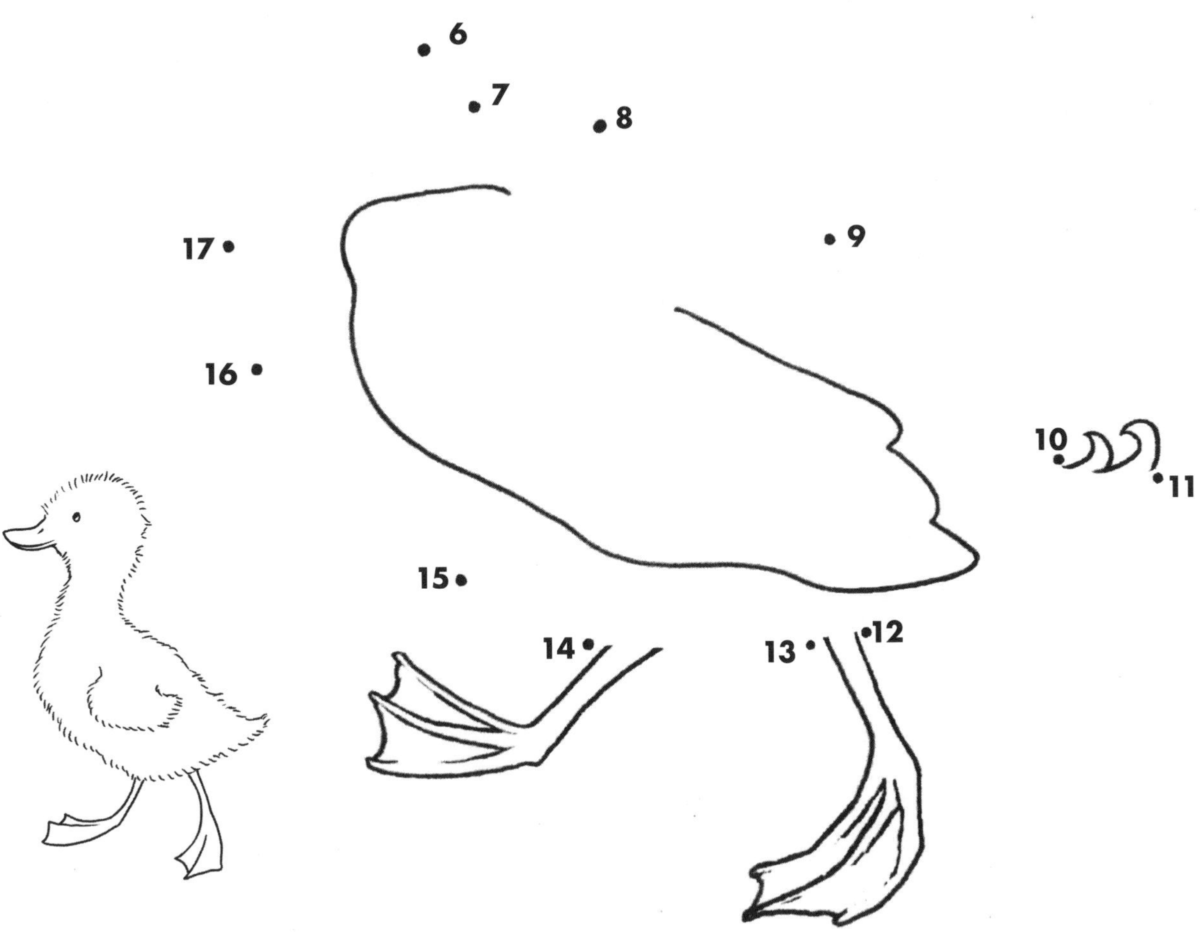

Colour the picture when you have finished.

Join the Dots (5)

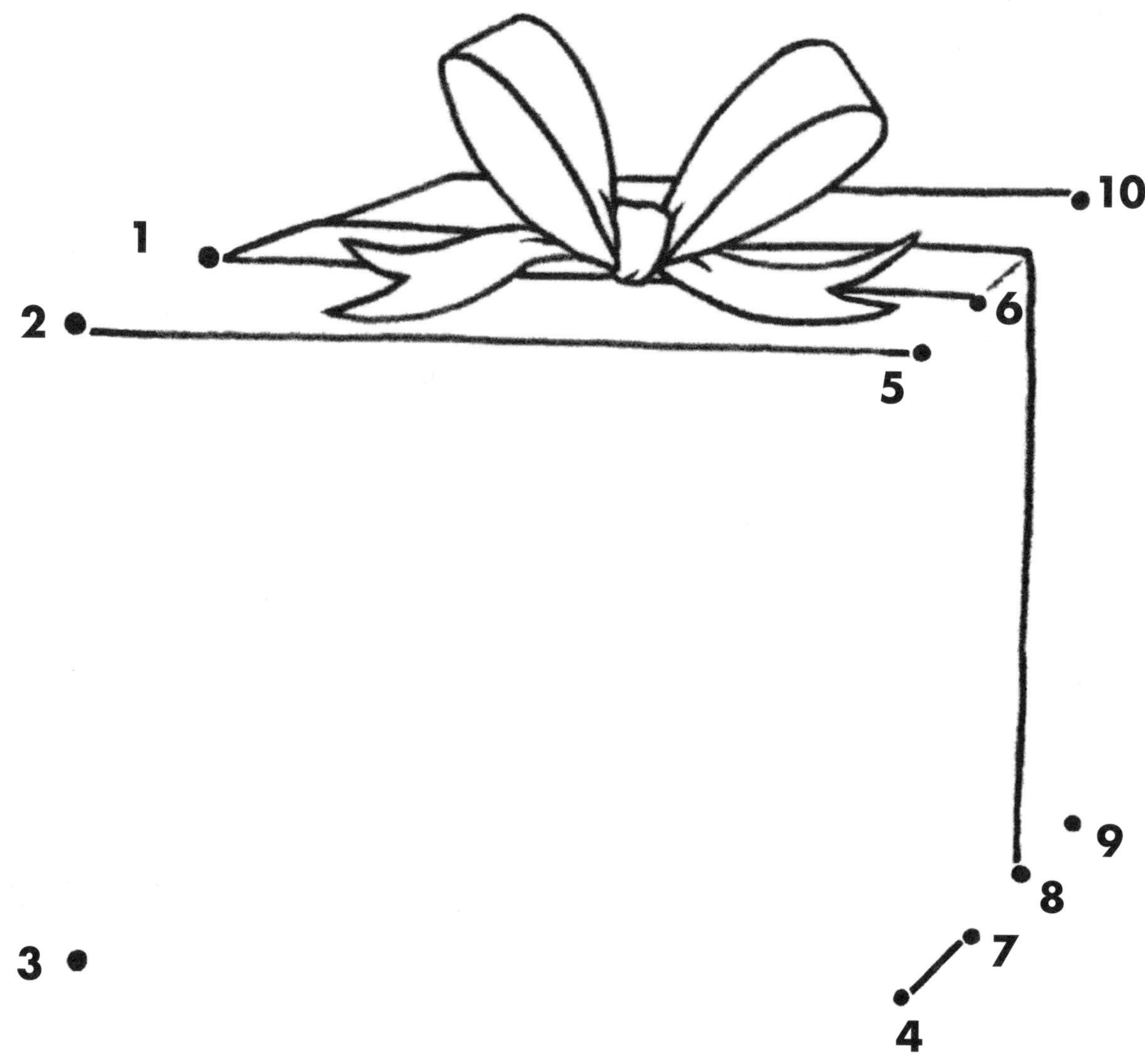

Draw some more parcels.

Now colour the picture.

      WET PLAY TODAY

Matching Pairs

Use a pencil line to match
up the pairs of things.

Missing Sportsman

Colour the picture to show the sportsman.

Half a Picture

Can you draw the missing
parts of this picture?

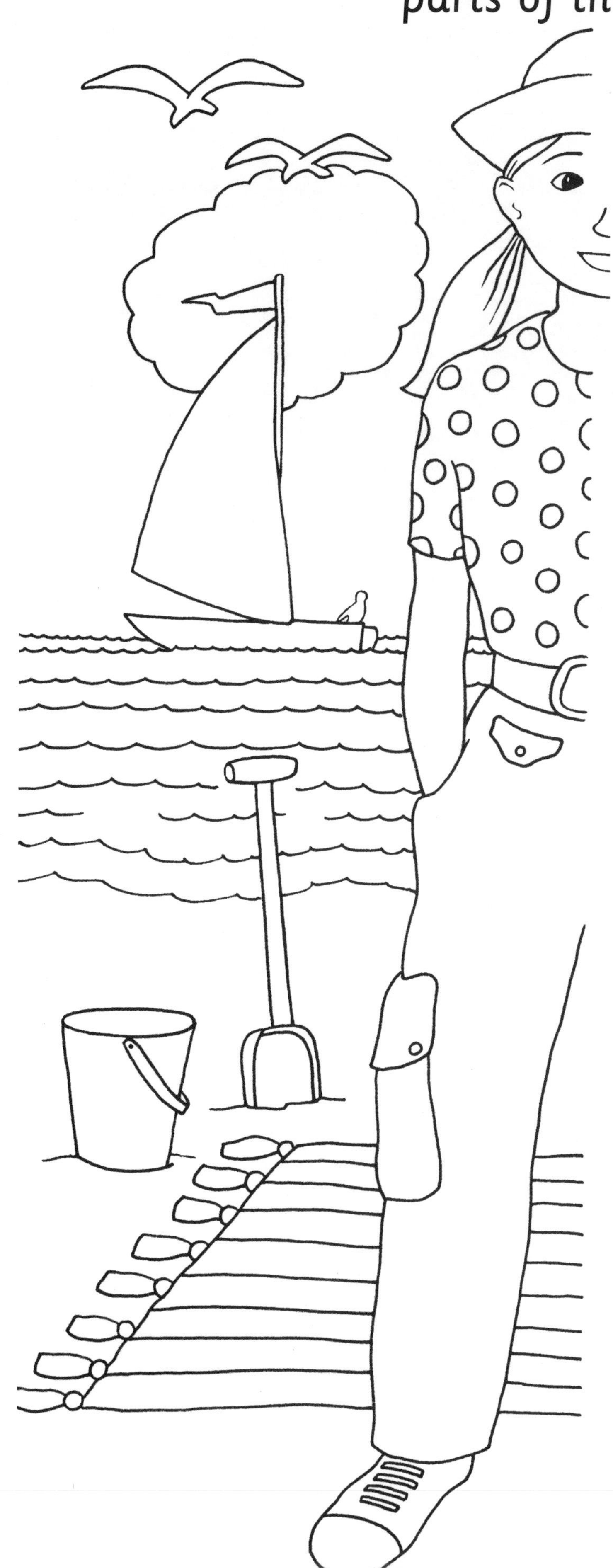

Picture Story

Draw in the
right pictures
to complete
the story.

Once upon a time, a little

□ lived in a dark □

near a big house. One day the

little □ was frightened by

a fat □ and fell into the

river.

 © Andrew Brodie Publications   www.acblack.com   WET PLAY TODAY

"Help!" cried the little mouse. A ☐ heard the little mouse and threw a ☐ to the little mouse. The little mouse held on to the stick and the girl pulled him to safety. The girl liked the little mouse so much that she said that he could come and live in the big ☐.

Missing Halves (1)

Spot the matching parts of the animals and then draw in the missing part of each one.

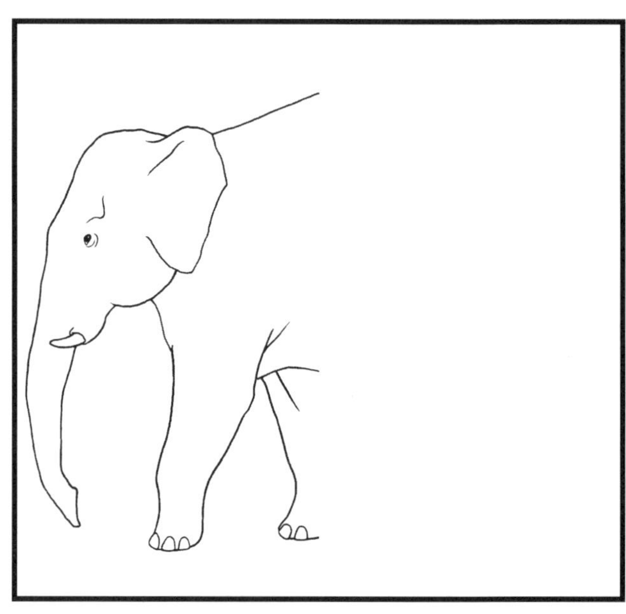

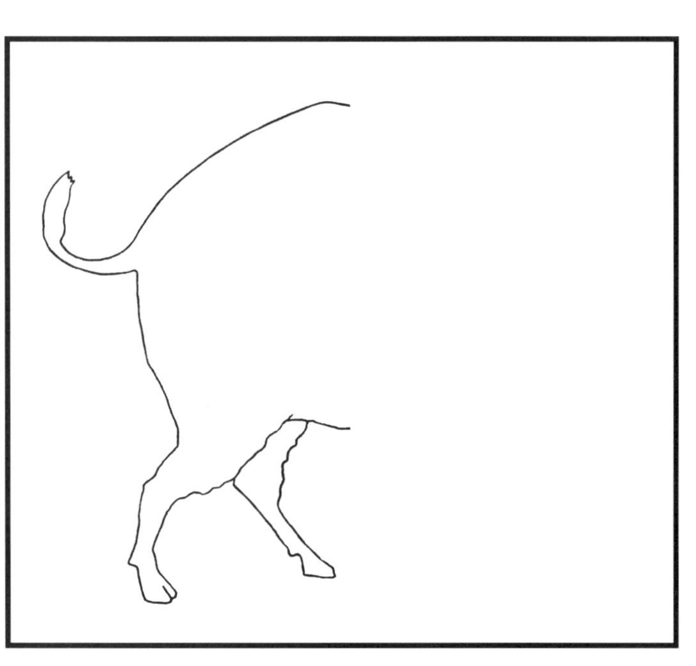

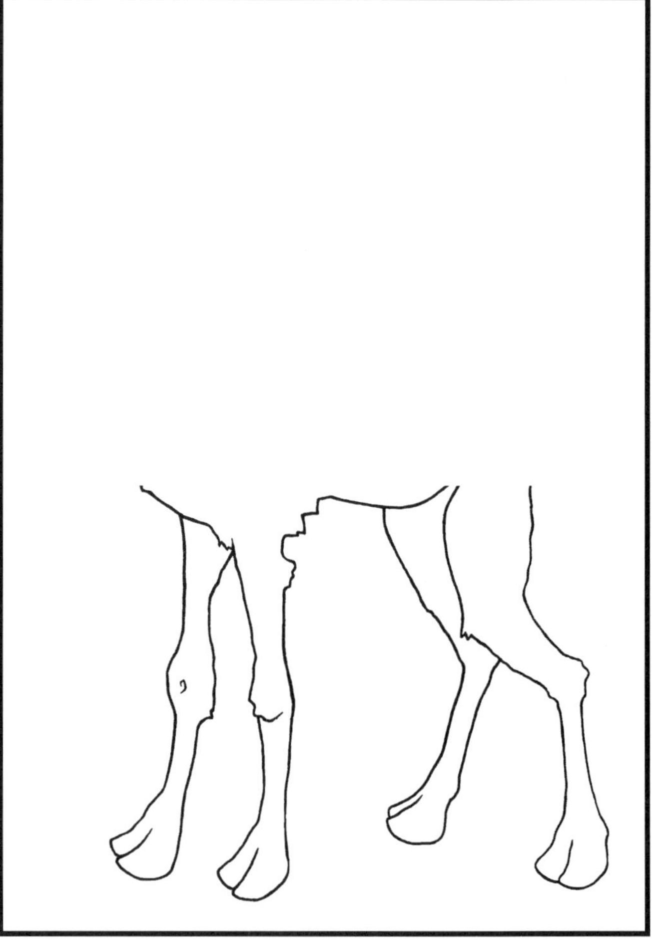

 © Andrew Brodie Publications www.acblack.com

Missing Halves (2)

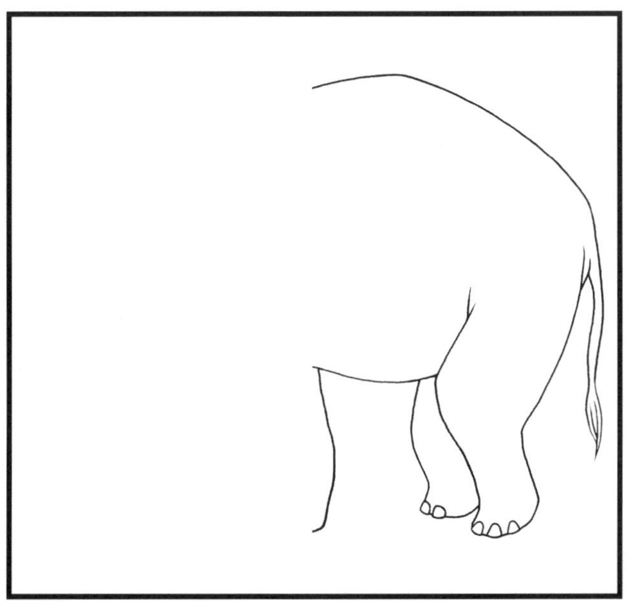

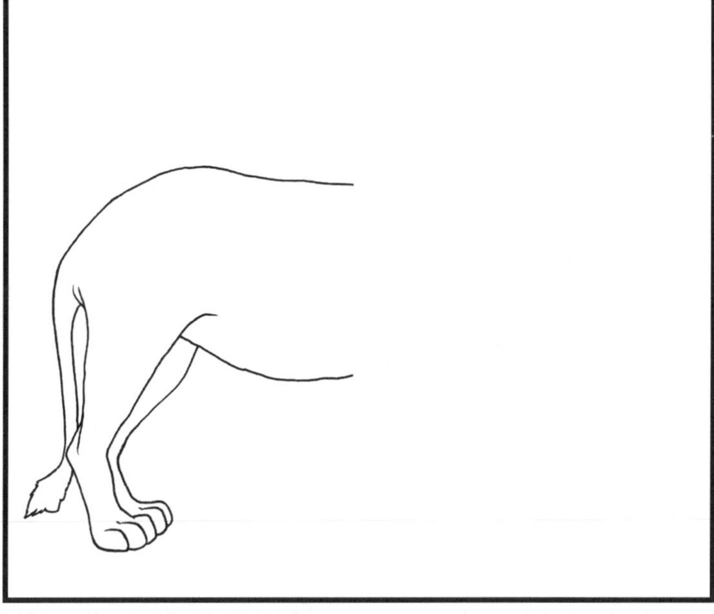

Two in One
Fold the paper along the lines, first one way, then the other. Open out to see two pictures.

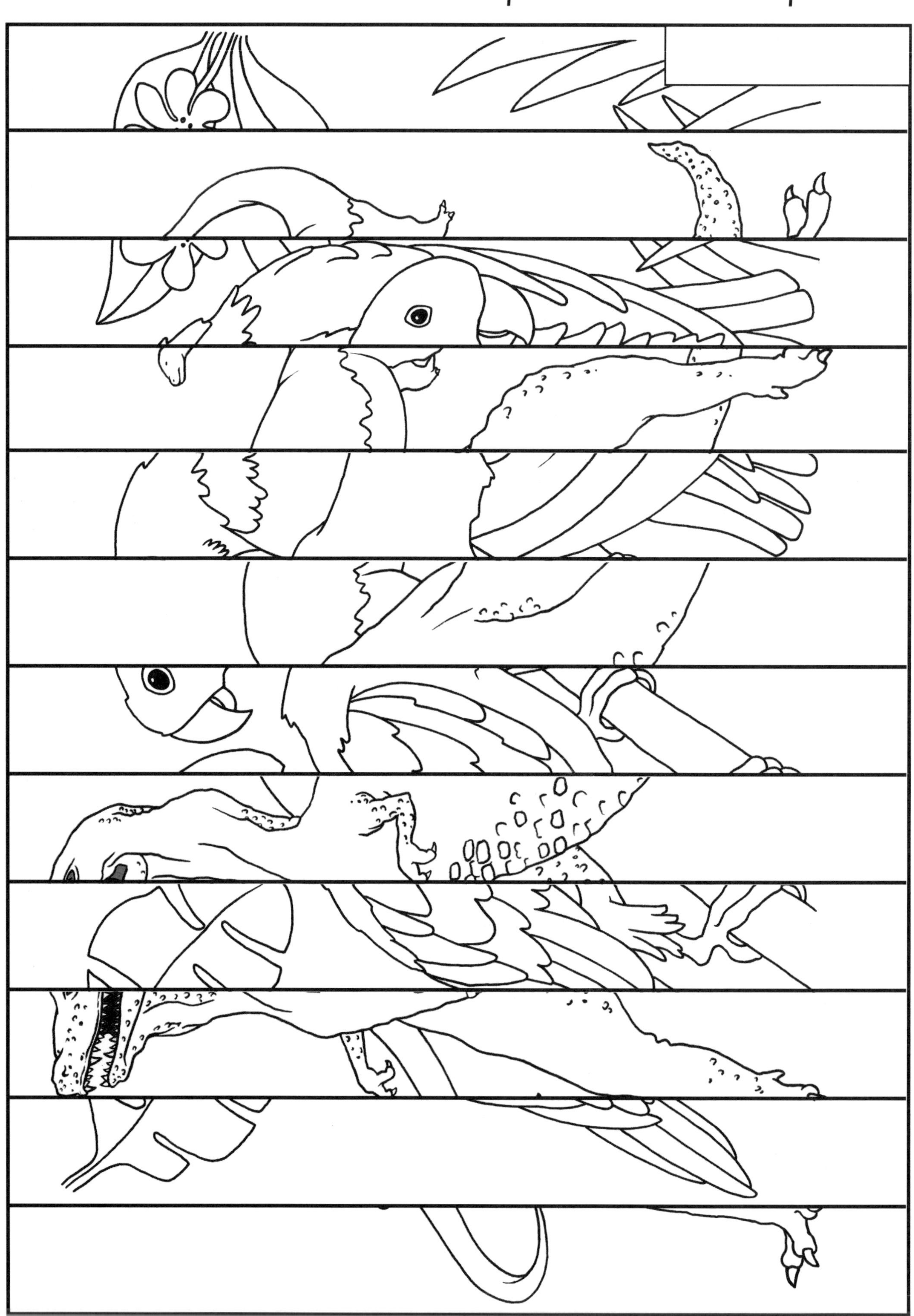

 © Andrew Brodie Publications   www.acblack.com   WET PLAY TODAY

Code Words

A	B	C	D	E	F	G	H	I	J	K	L	M
1	2	3	4	5	6	7	8	9	10	11	12	13

N	O	P	Q	R	S	T	U	V	W	X	Y	Z
14	15	16	17	18	19	20	21	22	23	24	25	26

Use the code to find these words:

| 3 | 1 | 20 | | _ _ _

| 2 | 15 | 1 | 20 | _ _ _ _

| 19 | 21 | 14 | _ _ _

Try writing some words of your own using the code.

| 6 | 1 | 20 | _ _ _

| 4 | 15 | 7 | _ _ _

Now try using this code:

A	B	C	D	E	F	G	H	I	J	K	L	M
26	25	24	23	22	21	20	19	18	17	16	15	14

N	O	P	Q	R	S	T	U	V	W	X	Y	Z
13	12	11	10	9	8	7	6	5	4	3	2	1

What do these words say?

| 25 | 26 | 25 | 2 | _ _ _ _

| 9 | 22 | 23 | _ _ _

| 23 | 6 | 24 | 16 | _ _ _ _

| 19 | 12 | 6 | 8 | 22 | _ _ _ _ _

| 11 | 12 | 13 | 23 | _ _ _ _

Try writing some words of your own using this code.

Super Spot

How many things can you spot that begin with the letter s?

© Andrew Brodie Publications   www.acblack.com

Rhyming Pairs

Can you find the four pairs of things that rhyme?
The first one has been done for you.

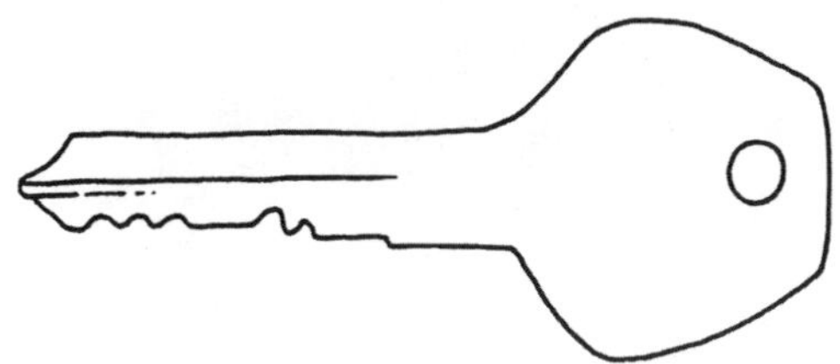

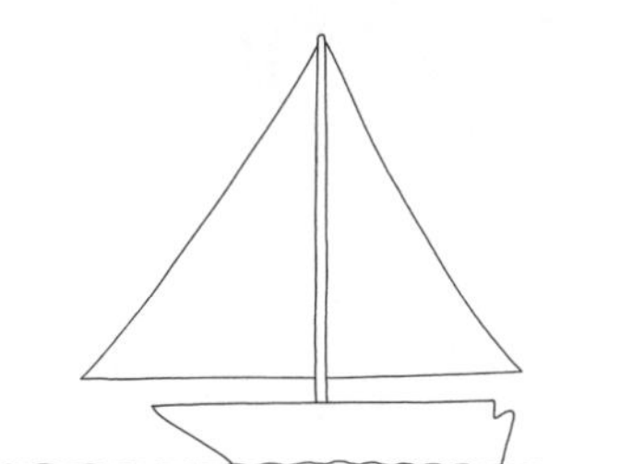

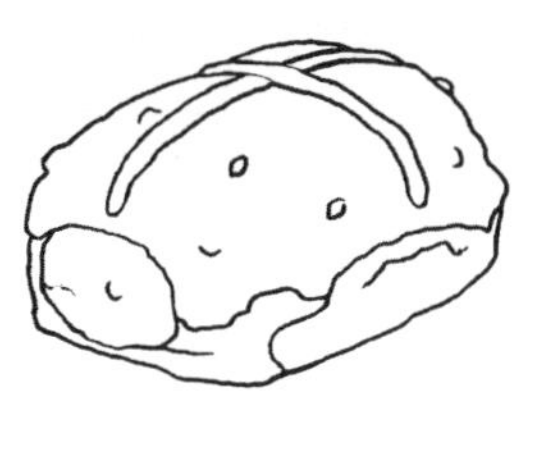

The words that rhyme are:

1   key and tree

2

3

4

Now you
can colour the
pictures.

Shadow Sports

Match up the sports figure with its shadow reflection.

Sports figure	1	2	3	4	5	6
Shadow						

      WET PLAY TODAY

Bit Fishy

Which fish doesn't have a twin?
Draw lines to join the twins and a
ring around the one without a twin.

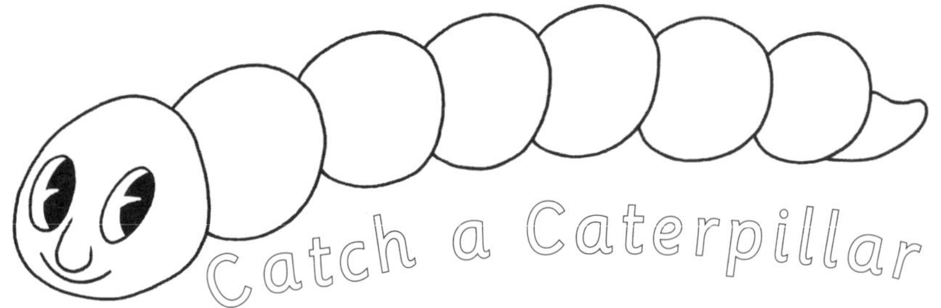

Catch a Caterpillar

A game for 2 people.   You will need one dice.

- Each of you should choose which is your caterpillar.
- Take it in turns to throw the dice.
- You are trying to throw the numbers on your caterpillar in the right order, starting with 1.
- When you throw a 1, you can colour in the 1 on your caterpillar.
- Now you need to throw a 2 and then you can colour that circle.
- Keep going until one of you has coloured in all the numbers on the caterpillar.

DON'T FORGET TO TAKE TURNS.

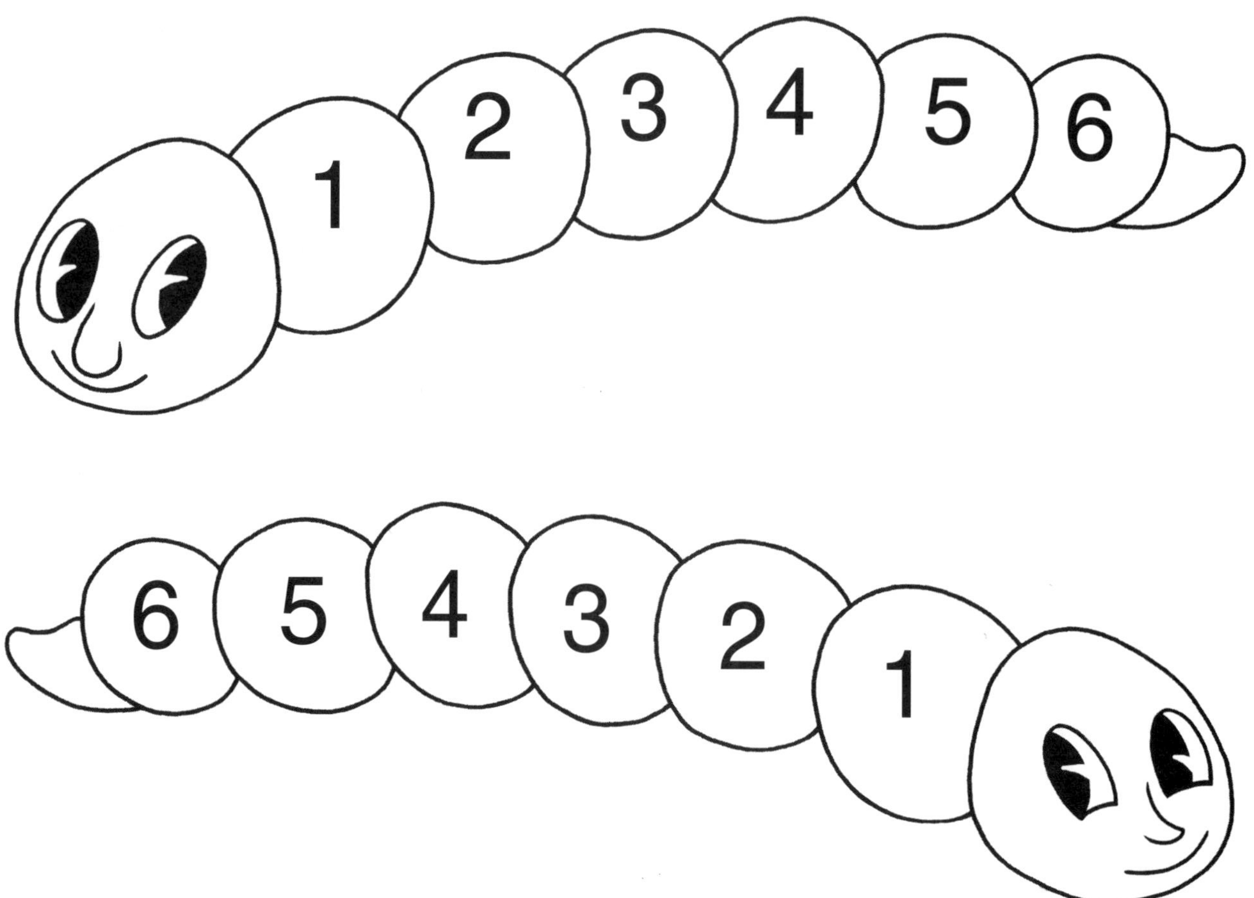

     WET PLAY TODAY

Muddled Characters

All these well known characters' names
have got muddled up.
Sort them out and then colour the pictures.

Robin Sprat

Robin _ _ _ _

Mary Dumpty

_ _ _ _ _ _ Dumpty

Jack Hood

Jack _ _ _ _ _

Snow Mary

_ _ _ _ Mary

Humpty Beauty

_ _ _ _ _ _ _ _ Beauty

Sleeping White

_ _ _ _ White

Who Lives Where?

Follow the lines to find the homes.
Use a different colour for each line.

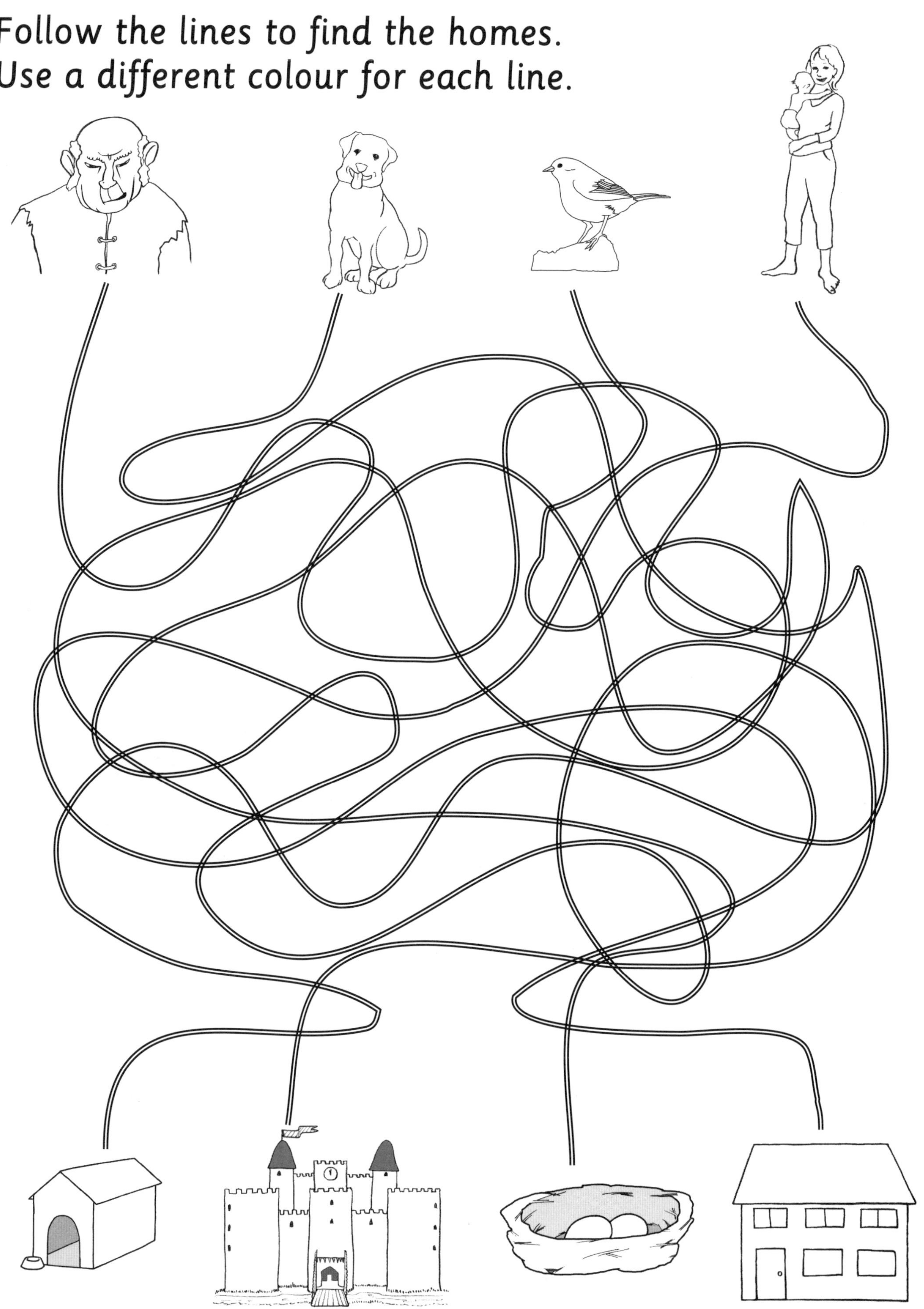

Write the second letter of the object in each picture to find the name of a bird. Here are the words you will need:

tractor   fish   astronaut   zebra   apple
sock   spoon   egg   brick   sun
car   snake   snowman   two

Write each second letter in here.

The bird is a   The bird is a

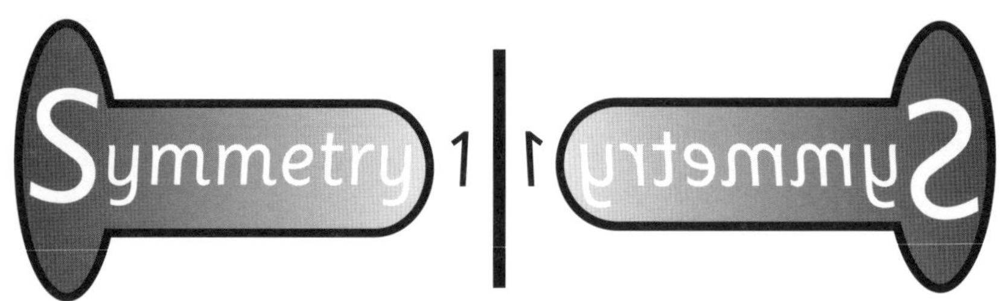

This pattern has symmetry;

Make this pattern have symmetry:

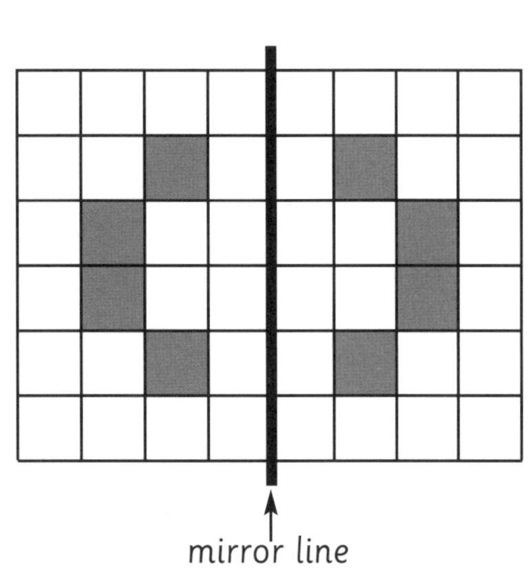

mirror line

Colour squares on this side... to match the squares on this side.

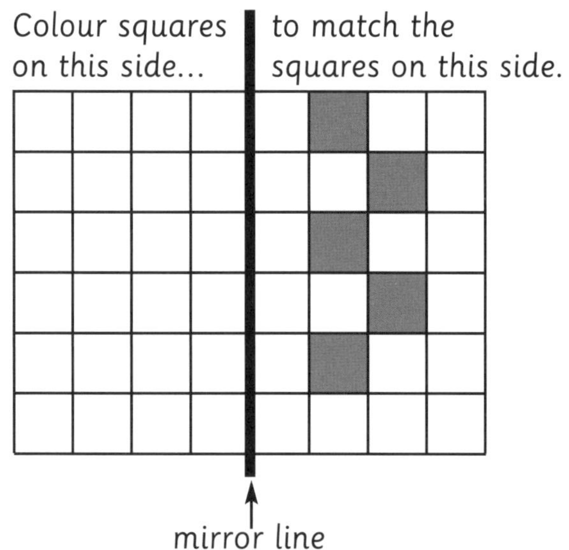

mirror line

Make these patterns have symmetry.

Colour squares on this side... to match the squares on this side.

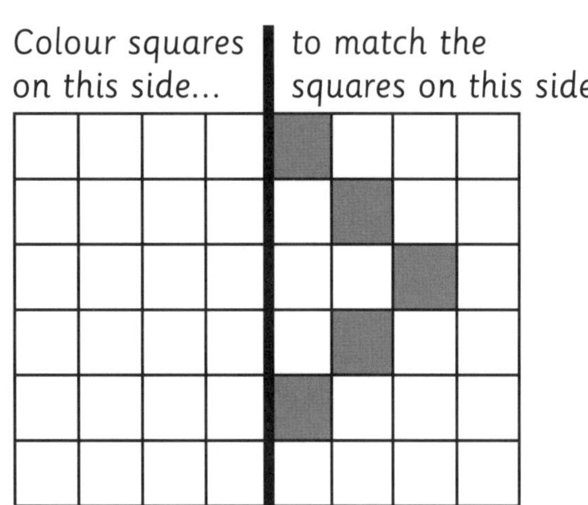

Colour squares on this side... to match the squares on this side.

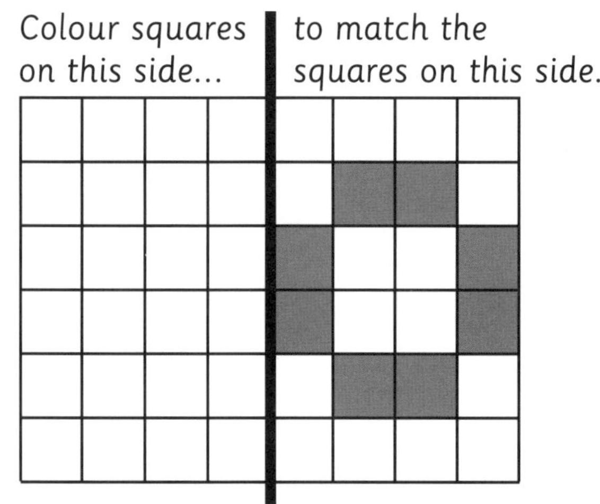

Colour squares on this side...

to match the squares on this side.

     WET PLAY TODAY

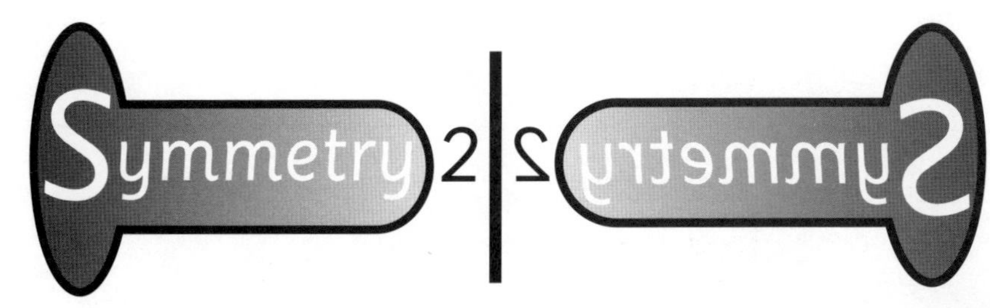

Make this pattern
have symmetry...

...by colouring
squares on this side.

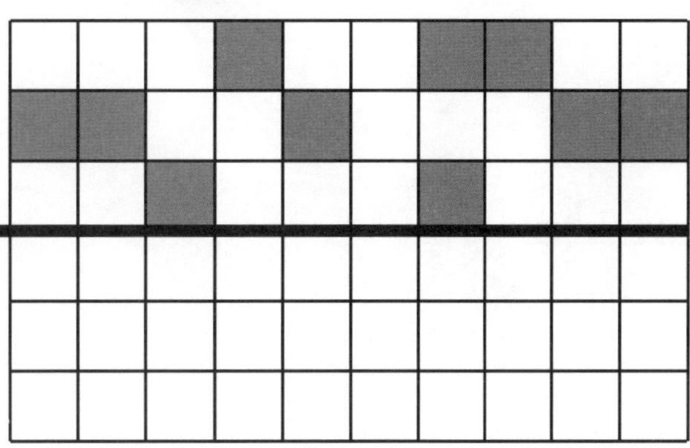

Colour the squares marked B blue.
R red
Y yellow

You have made
a pattern with
symmetry.

Make your own symmetrical pattern.

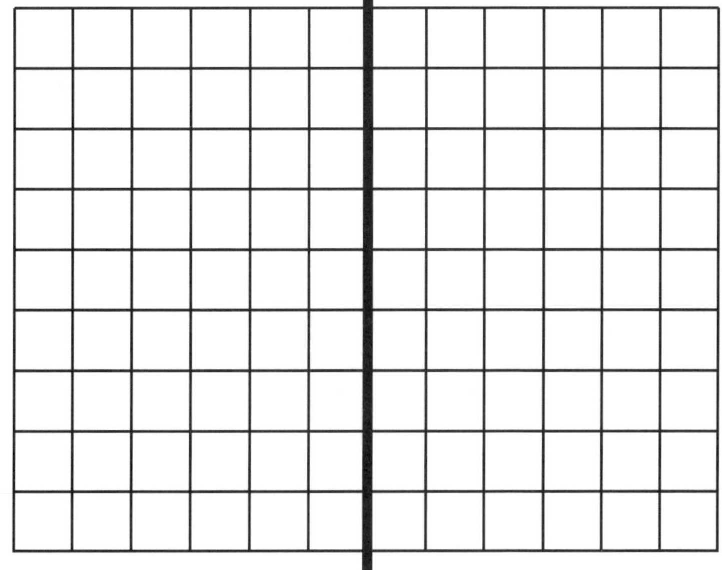

Wheels

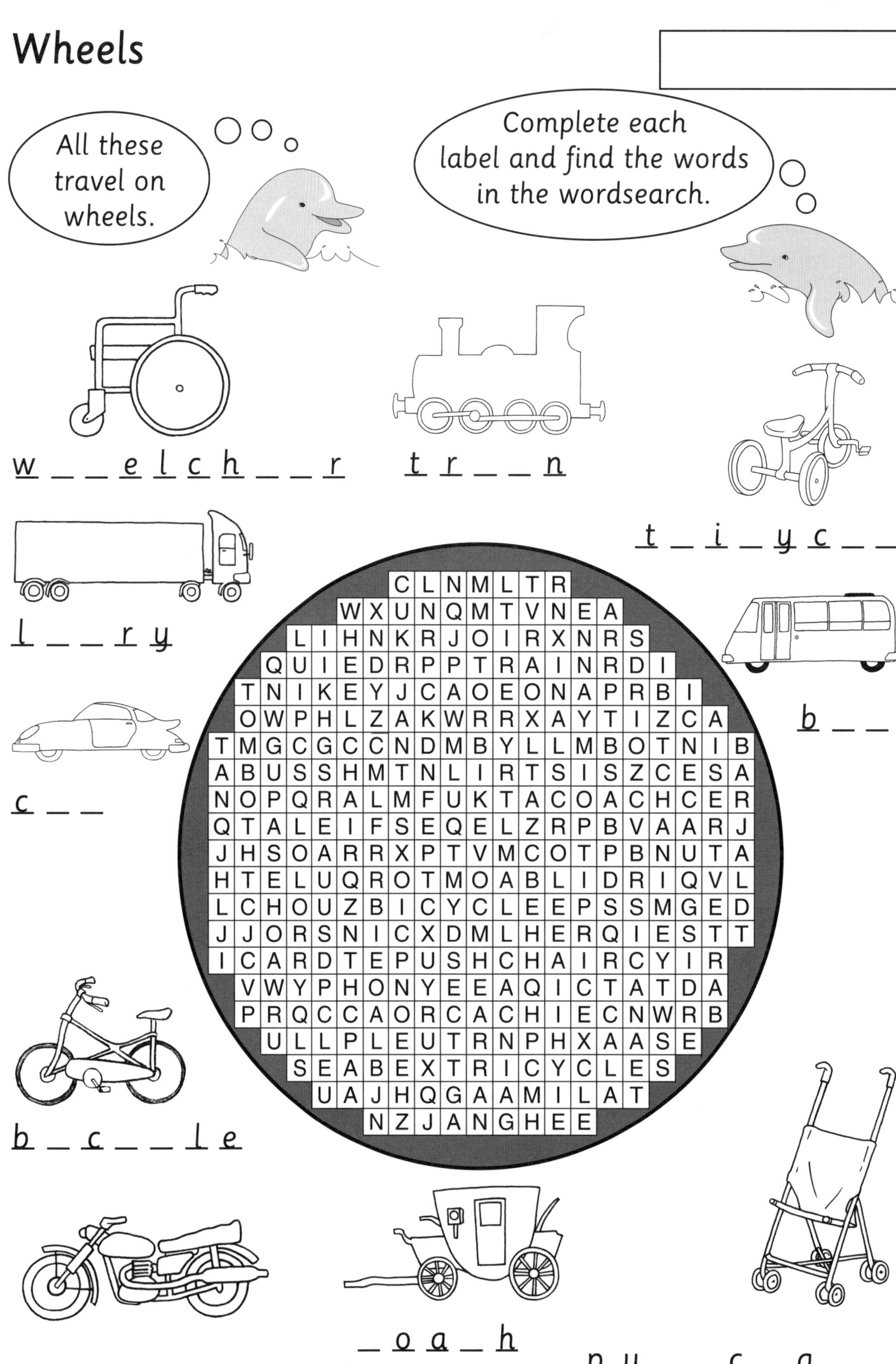

© Andrew Brodie Publications   www.acblack.com

Different Boys

Use these four colours to
make the boys different:

Red   Yellow   Blue   Green

Colour each boy's clothes so that every boy is dressed differently.
For example, the first boy could have a red T-shirt and yellow shorts.
Each piece of clothing must have only one colour.

Different Girls

Use these four colours to
make the girls different:

Red   Yellow   Blue   Green

Colour each girl's clothes so that every girl is dressed differently.
For example, the first girl could have a red T-shirt and yellow skirt.
Each piece of clothing must have only one colour.

   © Andrew Brodie Publications   www.acblack.com   WET PLAY TODAY

Odd Ones Out

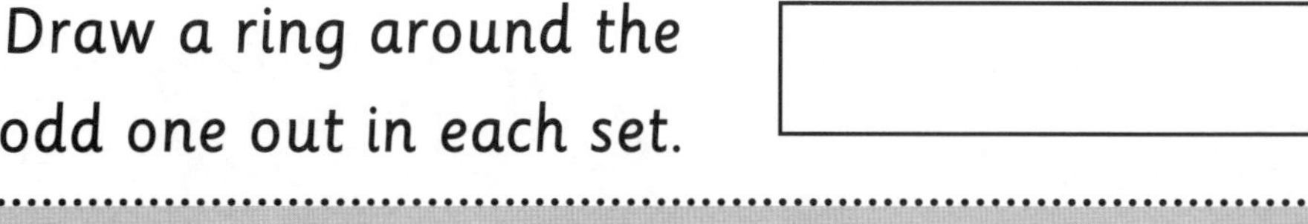

   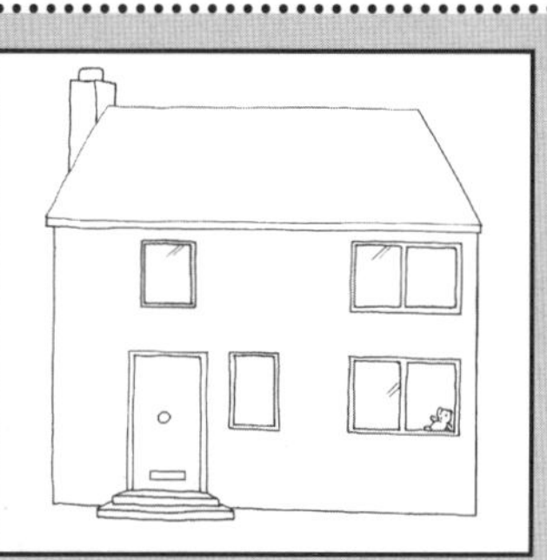

 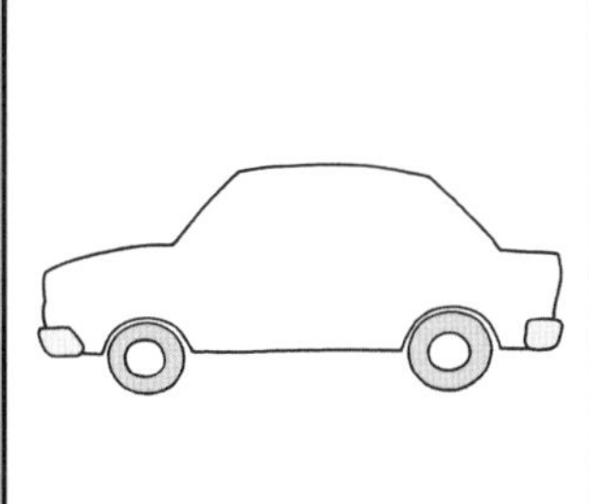  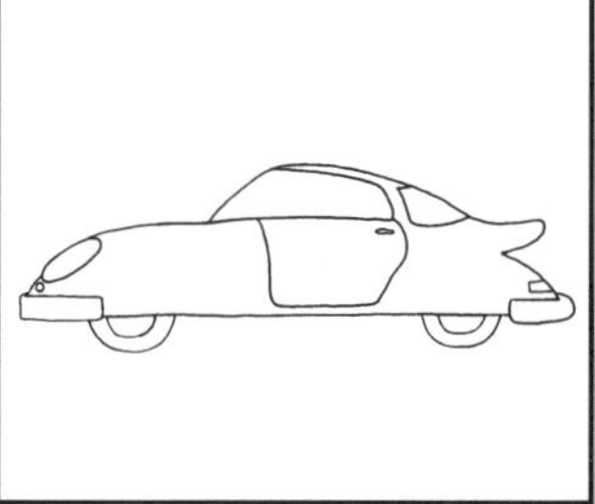

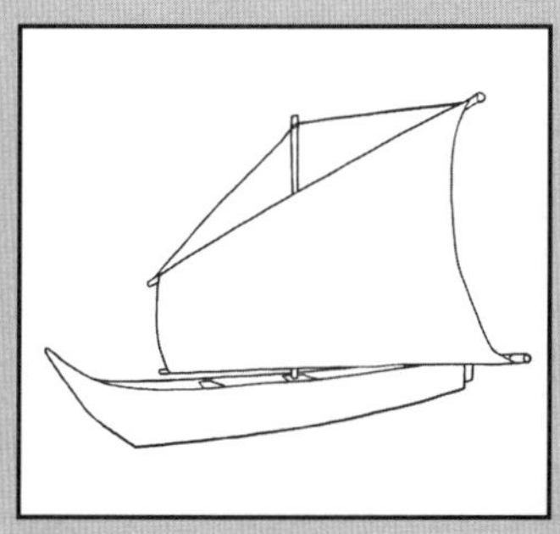  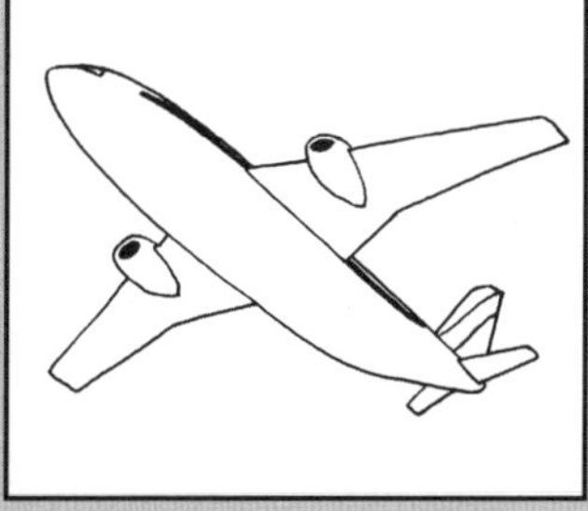 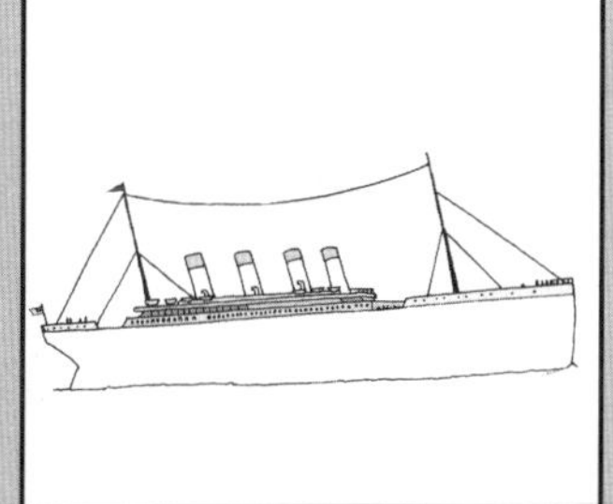

Now colour the pictures.

Musical Muddle 1

gtruia

____

ponia

____

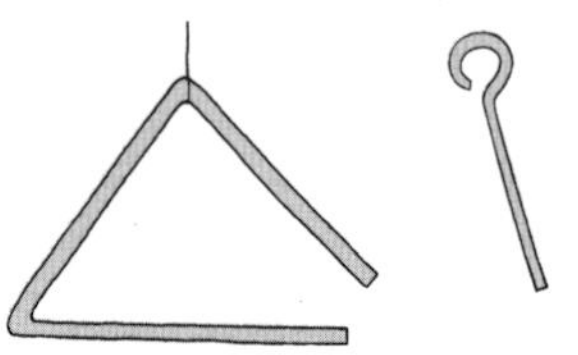

tirengla

____

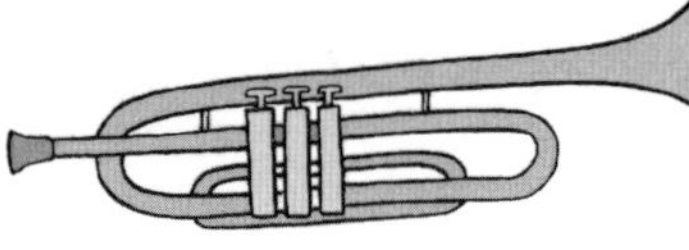

pretumt

____

viinlo

____

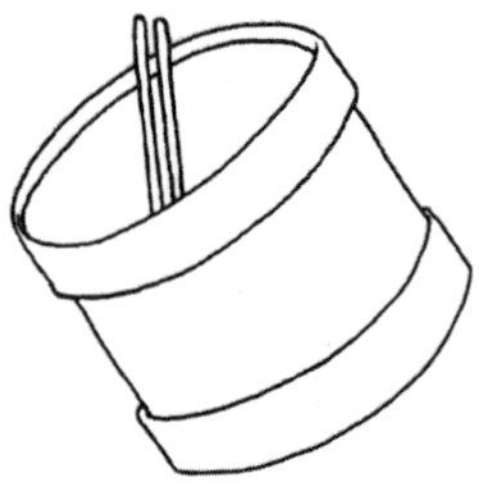

mudr

____

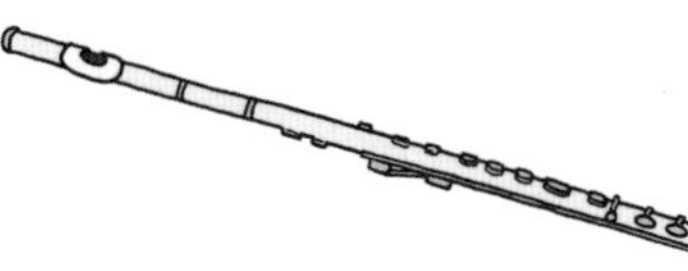

fleut

____

© Andrew Brodie Publications   www.acblack.com

WET PLAY TODAY

Musical Muddle 2

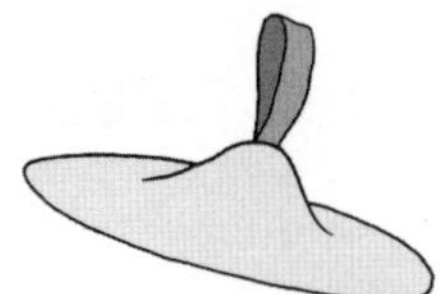

clymab

____

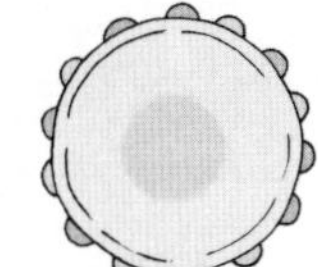

tibmuorane

____

soxephaon

____

a	t	a	m	b	o	u	r	i	n	e	h	a	o	x	h	t	w	l	u
f	p	q	b	m	w	k	a	t	e	j	g	x	l	n	d	r	u	m	o
h	p	i	a	n	o	o	n	z	o	o	r	l	k	q	f	u	n	t	c
m	y	d	k	q	g	u	i	t	a	r	i	o	w	c	y	m	b	a	l
o	v	w	k	z	u	s	i	e	m	e	o	s	q	p	s	p	o	l	e
p	a	i	g	e	h	u	w	a	b	k	s	e	v	o	l	e	a	r	m
i	s	a	x	o	p	h	o	n	e	p	a	w	i	m	f	t	g	y	p
a	s	k	r	b	z	o	w	m	s	a	l	s	o	x	y	w	y	c	
i	t	d	h	m	f	l	s	r	m	q	r	e	l	m	l	p	n		
	o	v	q	a	l	d	y	m	e	x	o	l	i	f	i	x			
		o	x	a	u	w	l	h	u	g	s	t	n	p	w				
			l	a	t	r	i	a	n	g	l	e	g	g					
			y	e	k	e	t	t	e	r	u	m	y						

To play this game you will need:
12 counters
1 die (numbered 1 to 6)

- Place 3 counters (these are your frogs) on a set of 3 frog pictures.

- Take it in turns to roll the die.

- Put one of your frogs on a lily pad showing the number you have thrown.

- If the lily pads showing your number have been covered, miss your turn.

- The winner is the first player to get all 3 of their frogs on to lily pads.

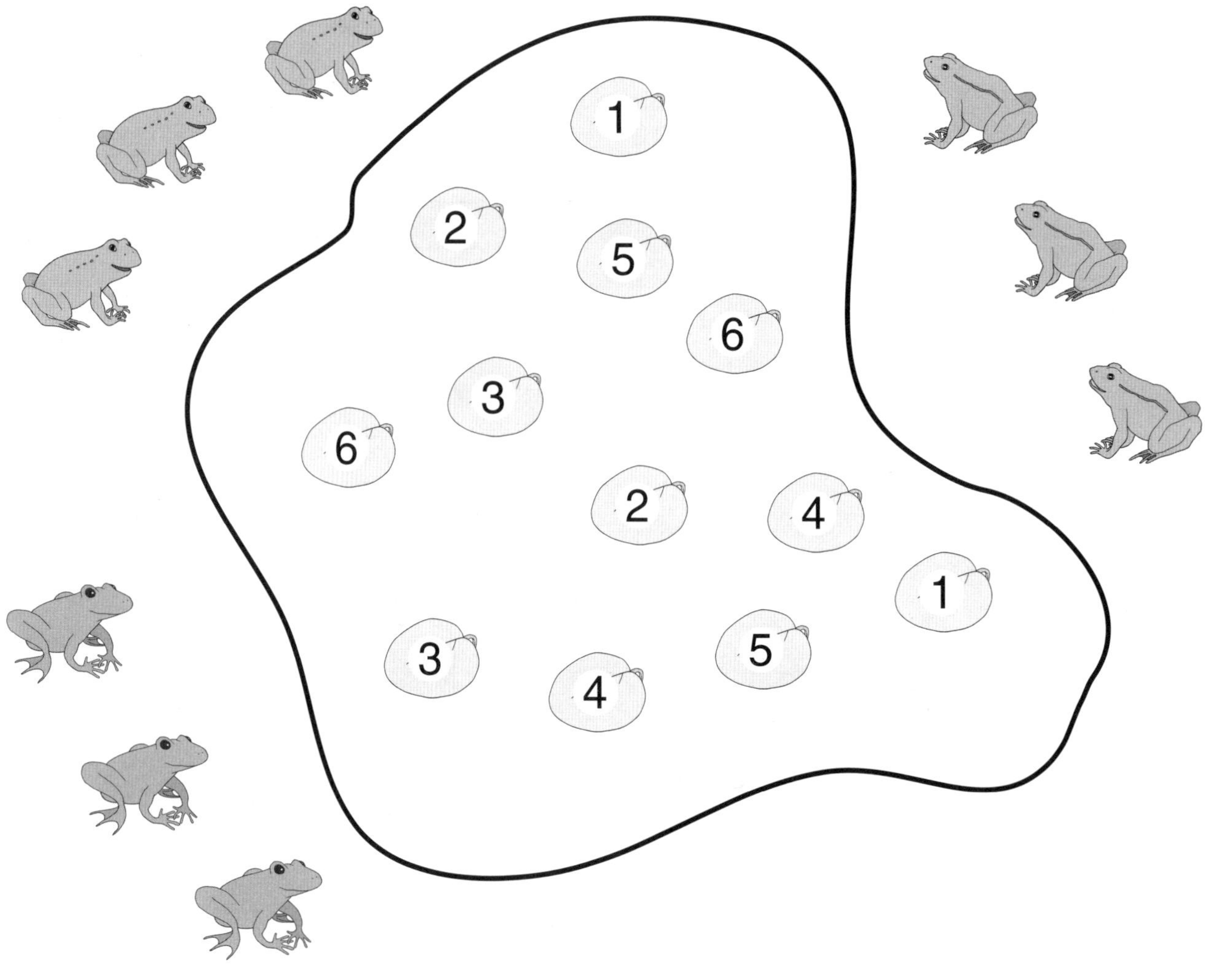

© Andrew Brodie Publications   www.acblack.com

First Past the Post

(a game for 2, 3 or 4 players.)

Holly, Bounty, Pandora and Star are having a race - you can help them.

<u>How to Play</u>

You will need: a counter for each player

a die numbered from 1 to 6

- Each player places a counter on their chosen horse.
- The die is rolled by each player in turn.
- To start on number 1, the number 1 must be rolled.
- After this, the numbers 2, 3, 4, 5 and 6 must be rolled in turn.
- The first one to reach the number six is the winner.

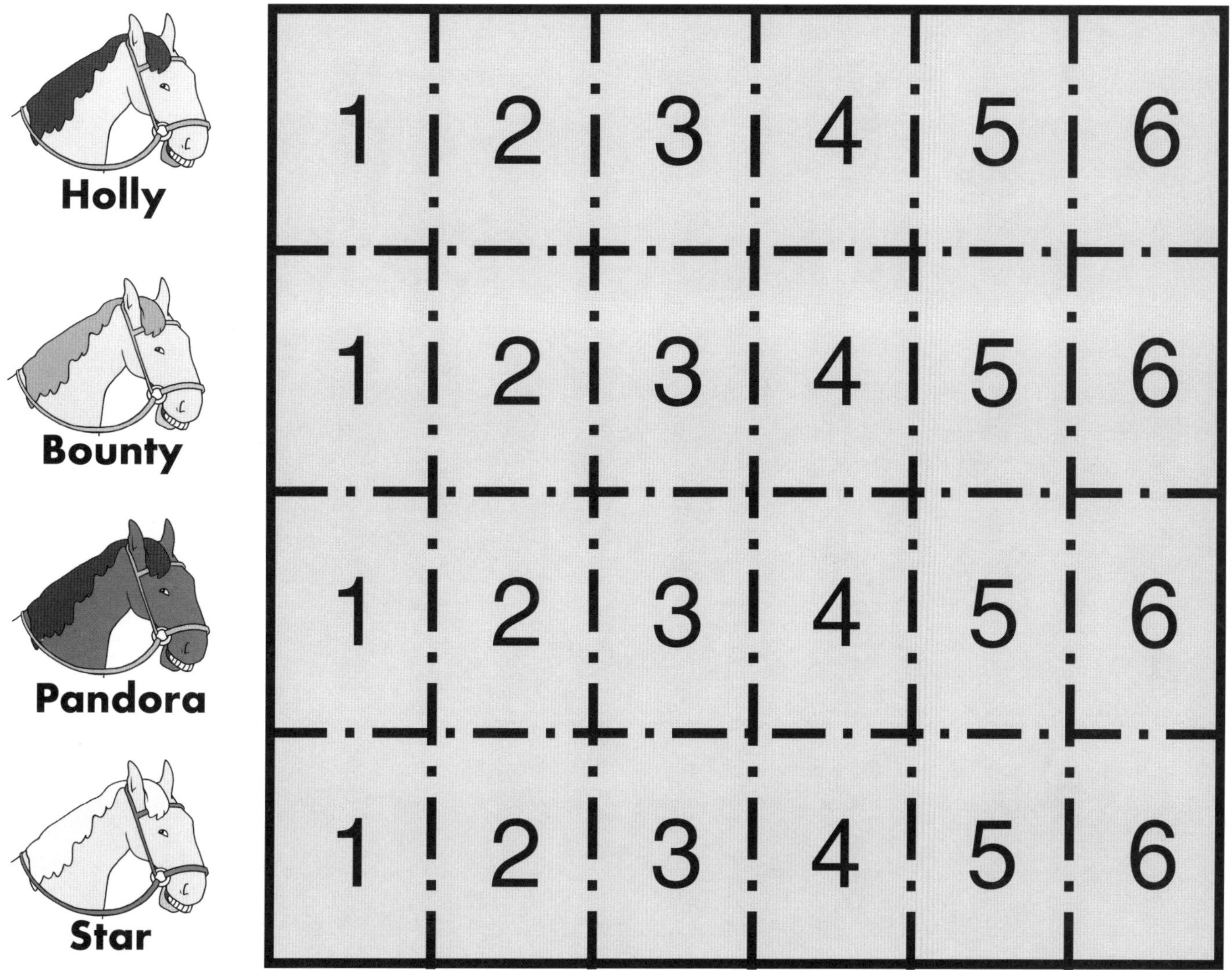

Be the first to give your fish 12 coloured bubbles.

You will need:　1 die marked 1 to 6
　　　　　　　　24 coloured counters

○ Place all counters in the bubble bank at the start of the game.
○ Take it in turns to roll the die.
○ If 1, 2, 3 or 4 is rolled, take one bubble from the bank for your fish.
○ If 5 is rolled, take one bubble from your fish and give it to the other player's fish (if you have one).
○ If 6 is rolled, take a bubble from the other player's fish and use it for your fish (if they have one).
○ The winner is the first to give their fish all 12 bubbles.

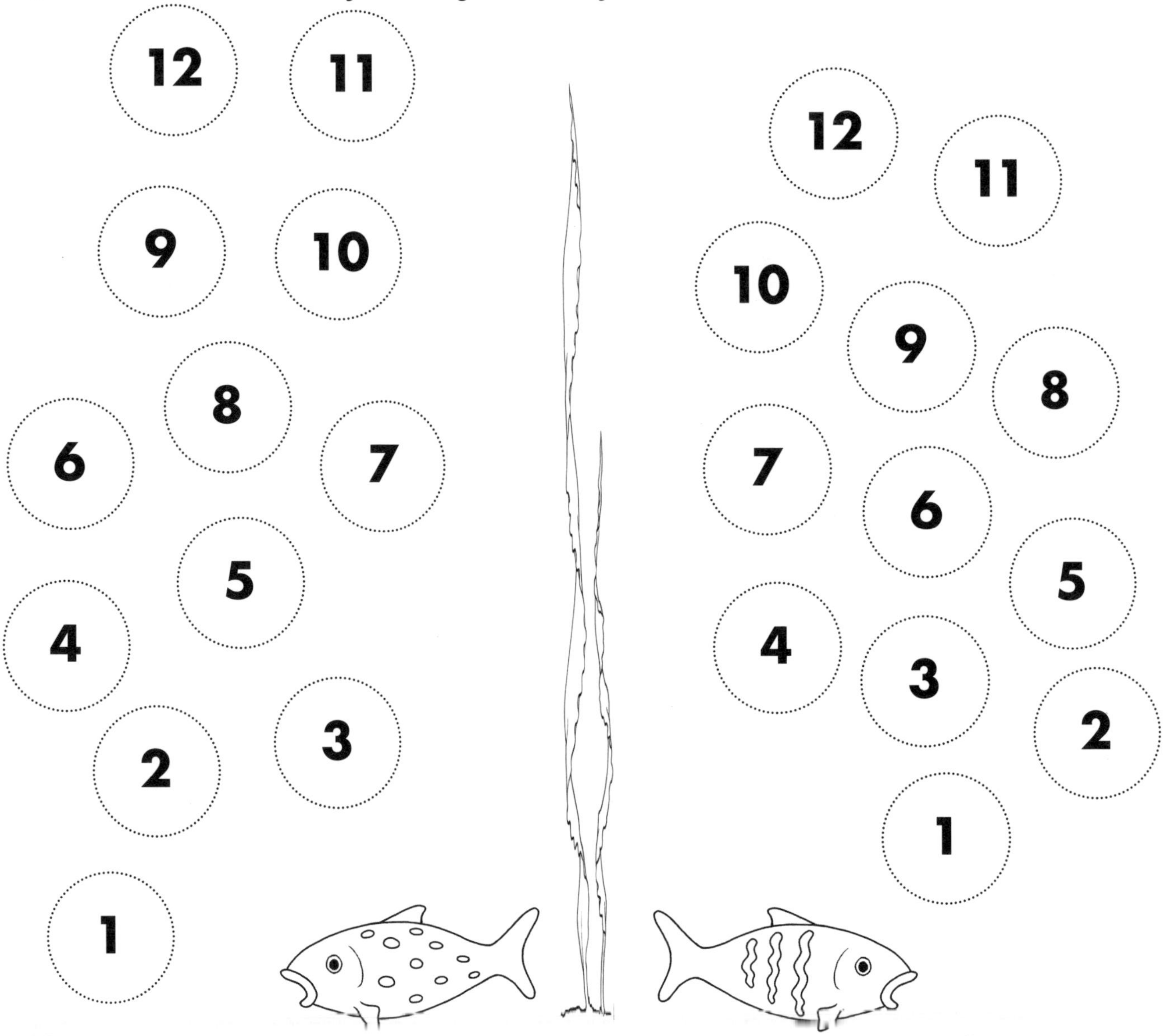

　© Andrew Brodie Publications　www.acblack.com　　WET PLAY TODAY

Load the Lorry (a game for 2 players)

You will need: 2 dice marked 1 to 6
coloured pencils

<u>How to Play</u>

- Each player chooses a lorry.
- Players take it in turns to roll both dice.
- One box is coloured - the box number must be either the number rolled on one of the die, or the total number of two dice added together.

  E.g. if [dice] and [dice] are thrown, you can colour 3, 4 or 7.

- If the scores rolled are already coloured, the player misses that turn.
- The winner is the first to have all their boxes coloured.

- -

Hidden Friends (1)

* ✳ Can you find the 16 nursery rhyme and fairy tale characters in this book?
* ✳ Use a coloured pencil to colour them in as you find them.
* ✳ The pictures are clues to help you.
* ✳ All the answers are written horizontally → or vertically ↓.

 © Andrew Brodie Publications   www.acblack.com

Hidden Friends (2)

z i w k s p f n o a l w o l p h b l a c c m a l x u m a
t h e b i l l y g o a t s g r u f f o i s g d t y l p i
s k s a i r e m x m n s o w p a n e r n l o i a n i w n
l i t t l e r e d r i d i n g h o o d d l l i a n t a c
l o l t l y g r e e n f i n g e l y e e a d s p l t d y
m a r y m a r y q u i t e c o n t r a r y i o u p l m w
i l b p a o x c n p w s l h d t u i l e y l v s c e j i
f a l i f j a e k x n i e o x n b c i l i o w s k b a n
c b r o t o m t h u m b m c a i o b t l n c i i o o p c
l z i e f g o a t f r o g y w o m t t a a k l n s p a y
l d i c k w h i t t i n g t o n i p l j p s f b c e b s
o a t g y a m m j e c d o k d o a p e l o w m o l e i p
m n i k f w h i t i g c j y i m t r b a y s i o x p p i
l i t t l e j a c k h o r n e r t r o w l c f t c u p d
k i n y m s l e e p i n g b e a u t y l l e s s f f o e
l i c k n o s r a c y t t e h d n a b y d n e w r o f r
h o l d m o t h e r h u b b a r d w l a s a n e r r a k
e r e e r a e n i f e r a l c a e s u u o h r e t r a h
q e u l b r u l b n e d r a g g a v e a s n o t n i h c
s n o w w h i t e a n d t h e s e v e n d w a r f s w r
u r e e n s a d c i n t h a i p a v n n y b e p a y e a
f h o p l i t t l e m i s s m u f f e t s r e d n e t s

© Andrew Brodie Publications   www.acblack.com

Sparkling Sportsmen
A game for 2, 3 or 4 players.

You will need: a die marked 1 to 6
                   coloured pencils

1 = black   2 = lilac   3 = blue   4 = yellow   5 = green   6 = red

- Choose one sportsman each.

- Take turns to roll the die.

- For each roll of the die colour one segment of your figure the correct colour. For example on a roll of 2, you may colour one sock.

- If you have already coloured the pieces that match the number rolled you have to miss a turn.

The winner is the first person to complete their sportsman.

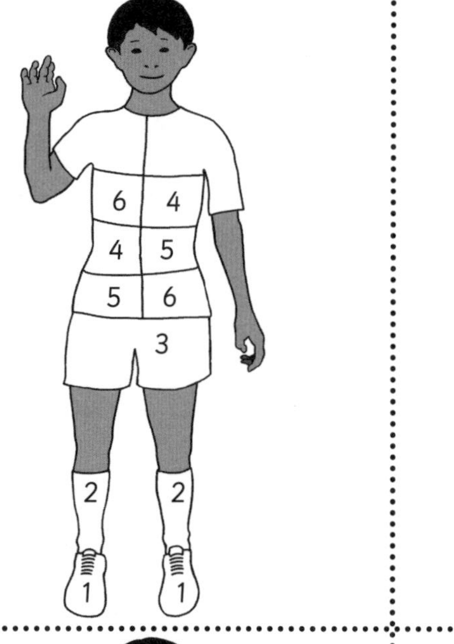

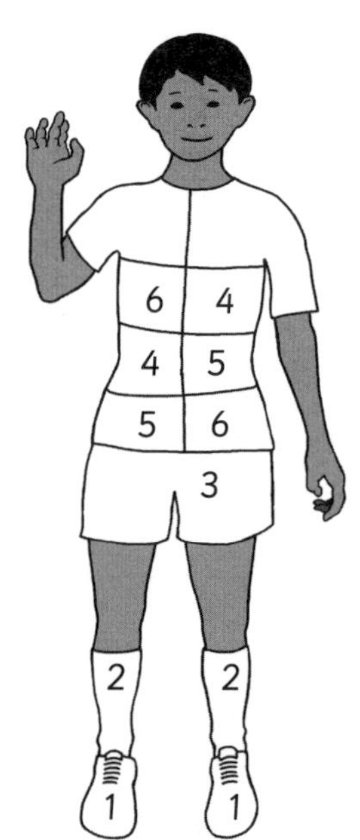

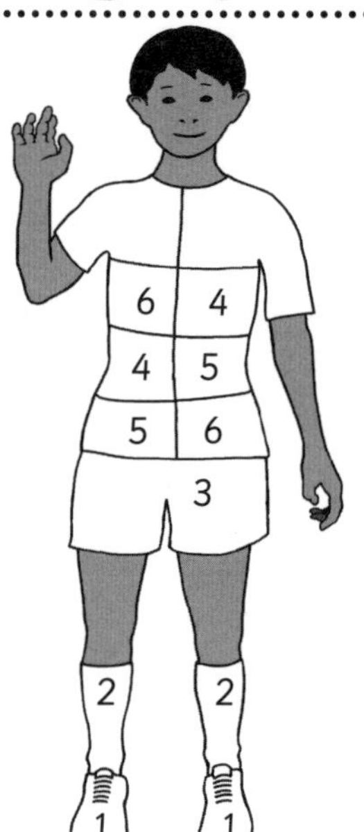

  © Andrew Brodie Publications   www.acblack.com   WET PLAY TODAY

Sparkling Sportswomen
A game for 2, 3 or 4 players.

You will need: a die marked 1 to 6
                     coloured pencils

1 = black   2 = lilac   3 = blue   4 = yellow   5 = green   6 = red

- Choose one sportswoman each.

- Take turns to roll the die.

- For each roll of the die colour one segment of your figure the correct colour. For example on a roll of 2, you may colour one sock.

- If you have already coloured the pieces that match the number rolled you have to miss a turn.

The winner is the first person to complete their sportswoman.

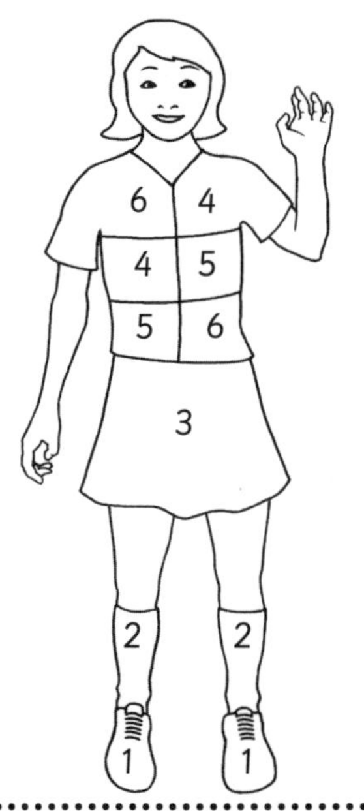

Fairy Tales and Nursery Rhymes

Use the missing words from the Fairy Tale and Nursery Rhyme titles to complete the word puzzle.
Some of the answers go across and some go down.

Clues Across

1. Puss in _ _ _ _ _ _ .
2. Jack _ _ _ the beanstalk.
5. Incy Wincy _ _ _ _ _ _ _.
6. Old _ _ _ _ _ _ _ Hubbard.
8. The three little pigs and the big bad _ _ _ _.
9. _ _ _ _ _ _ _ Boy Blue.

Clues Down

1. Goldilocks and the three _ _ _ _ _ _ .
3. Mary Mary Quite _ _ _ _ _ _ _ _ _.
4. Jack and Jill _ _ _ _ up the hill.
6. Little Miss _ _ _ _ _ _ _.
7. Little Red Riding _ _ _ _.

 © Andrew Brodie Publications   www.acblack.com

Classroom Capers (1)

Oh dear, my classroom labels have the
letters in the wrong order. Can you help to unjumble them?

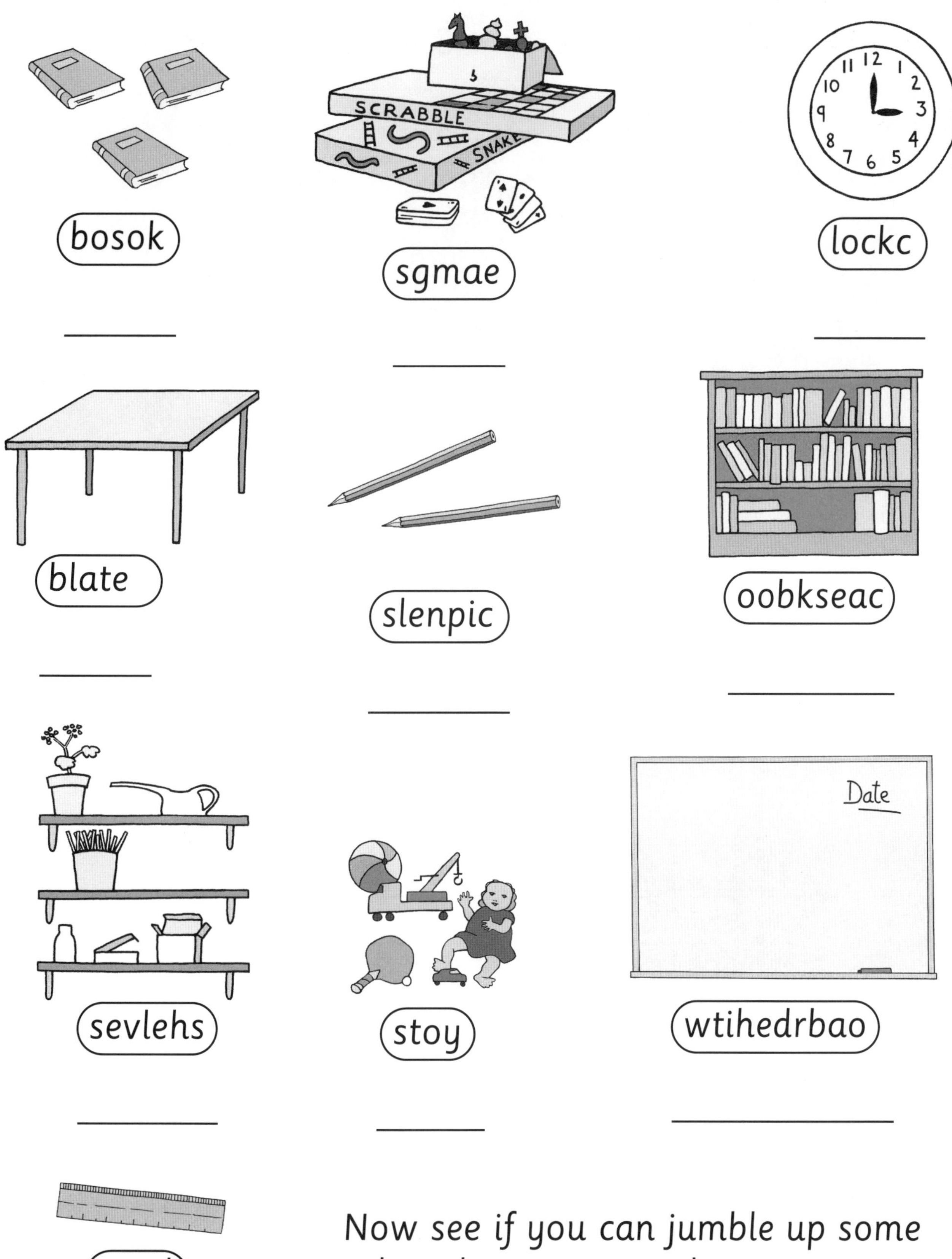

Now see if you can jumble up some
other classroom words.
See if a friend can unjumble them.

Classroom Capers (2)

These are all things you might see in your classroom.
Can you find them in the wordsearch?
All the words will be found written horizontally ➝ or vertically ↓.

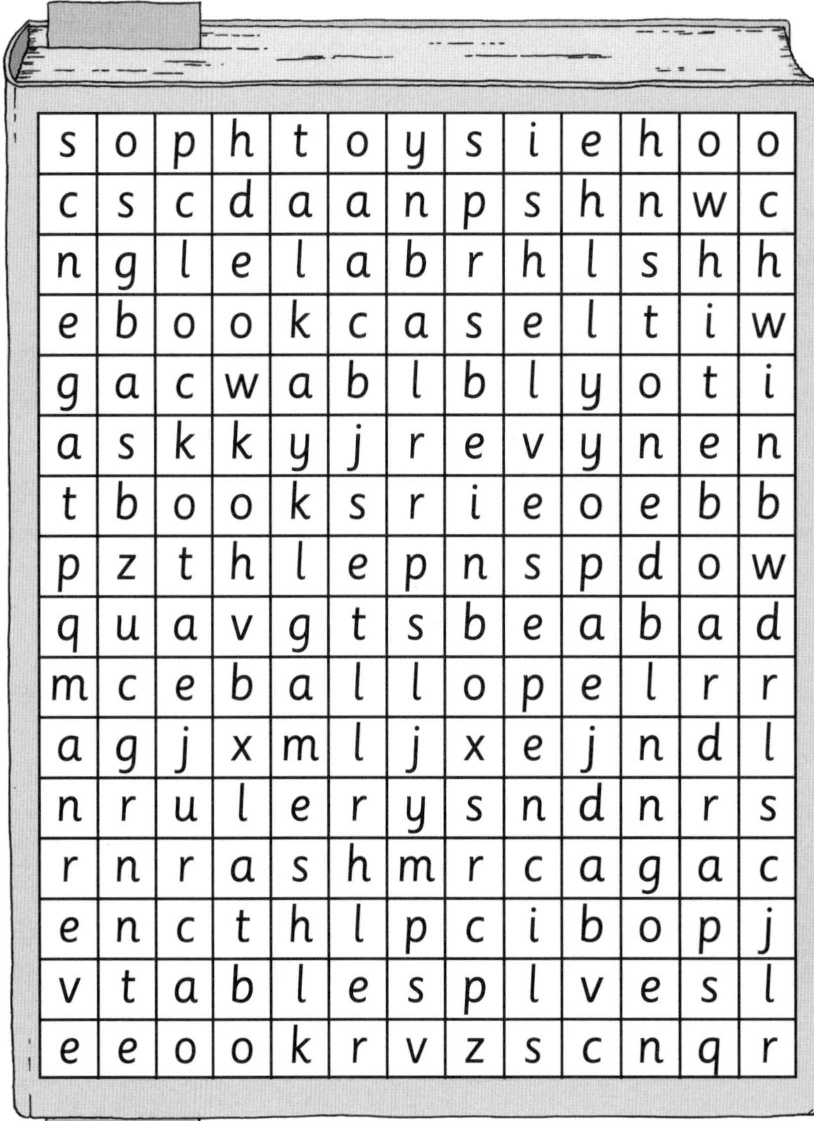

© Andrew Brodie Publications   www.acblack.com

WET PLAY TODAY

Snakes, Ladders and Clouds

You will need a counter for each person and a die numbered 1 to 6.

Throw the die and move your counter the same amount as the number on the die. If you land on a ladder, you can go up it. If you land on a snake you must go down it. If you land on a cloud you must follow the instructions on it.

The winner is the first person to reach 100.

100	99	98	97	96		94	93	92	91
81	82	83	84	85	86	87	88	89	90
80	79	78	77		75	74	73	72	71
61	62	63		65	66	67	68		70
60	59	58	57	56	55	54	53	52	51
41	42	43	44	45	46	47	48	49	50
40	39	38	37	36	35	34	33	32	31
21	22	23	24	25	26	27	28	29	30
20	19	18	17	16	15	14	13	12	11
1	2	3	4	5	6	7	8	9	10

Draw It - Butterfly

Draw here or on scrap paper. Now try again.

Now colour them all in.

Draw It - Cat

Draw here or on scrap paper. Now try again.

Now colour them all in.

Draw It - Elephant

Draw here or on scrap paper. Now try again.

Now colour them all in.

  © Andrew Brodie Publications   www.acblack.com   WET PLAY TODAY

Draw It - Owl

Draw here or on scrap paper. Now try again.

Now colour them all in.

Draw It - Teddy

Draw here or on scrap paper. Now try again.

Now colour them all in.

     WET PLAY TODAY

Colour Pattern (1)

Use these colours:
R = red
G = green
B = blue

R	R	R	R	R	R	R	R	G
R	G	B	G	B	G	B	R	B
R	B	R	R	R	R	G	R	G
R	G	R	G	B	R	B	R	B
R	B	R	B	R	R	G	R	G
R	G	R	G	B	G	B	R	B
R	B	R	R	R	R	R	R	G
R	G	B	G	B	G	B	G	B
R	R	R	R	R	R	R	R	R

Colour Pattern (2)

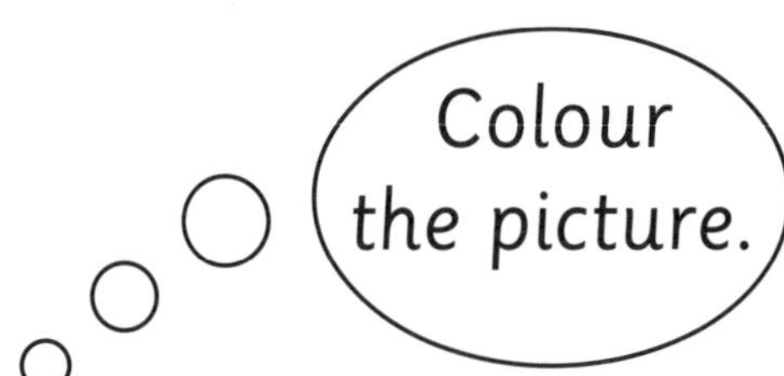

Use these colours:
R = red
G = green
B = blue

G	B	R	G	R	G	R	B	G
B	R	G	R	B	R	G	R	B
R	G	B	G	R	G	B	G	R
G	R	G	B	G	B	G	R	G
R	B	R	G	R	G	R	B	R
G	R	G	B	G	B	G	R	G
R	G	B	G	R	G	B	G	R
B	R	G	R	B	R	G	R	B
G	B	R	G	R	G	R	B	G

     WET PLAY TODAY

Repeating Patterns (1)

Colour the sheet if you want to.

Repeating Patterns (2)

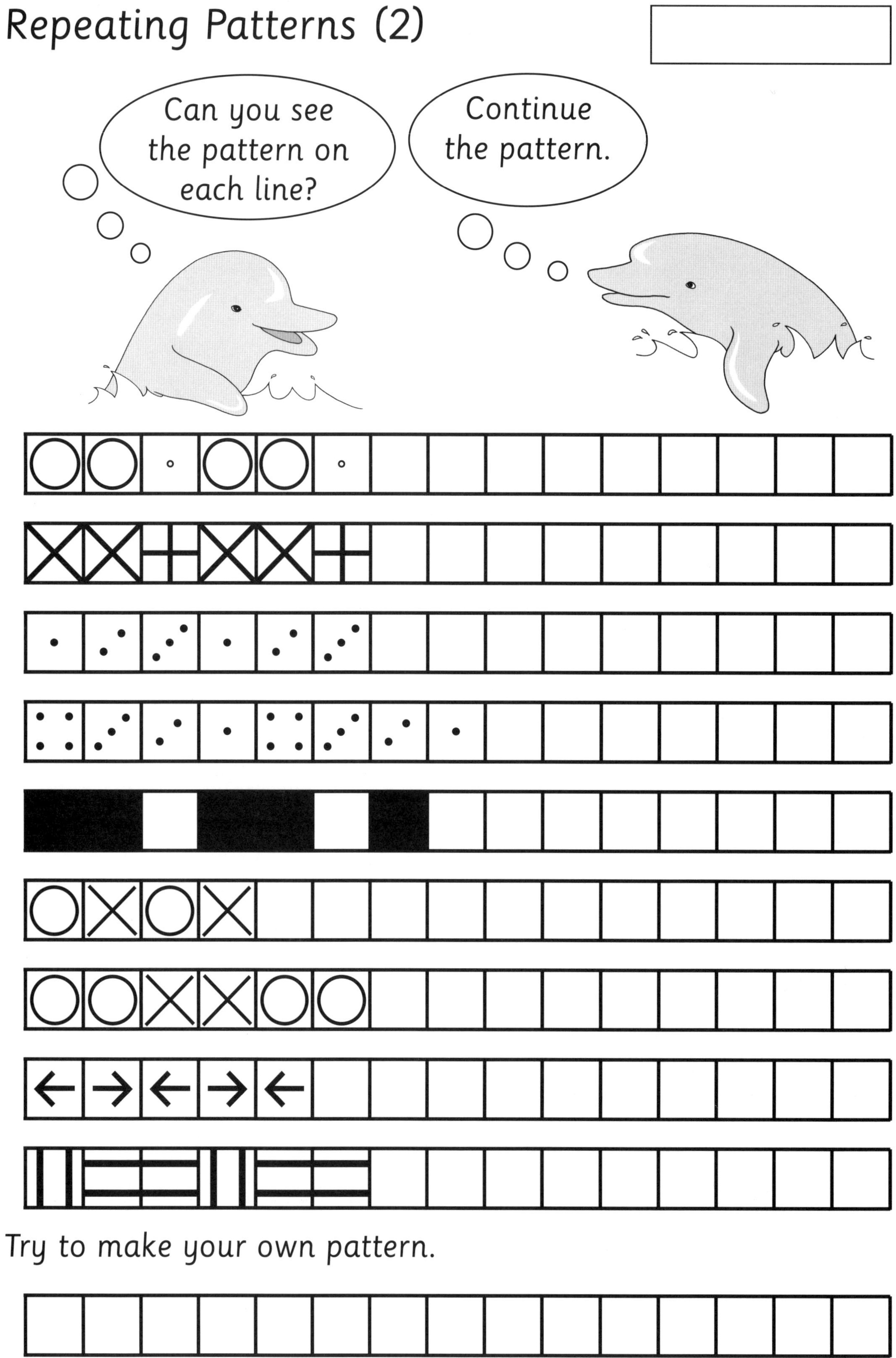

Try to make your own pattern.

Follow the Trails

Follow the dog's trail.
Colour the squares on his path in blue.
Now follow the other trails.
Colour the cat's path red.
Colour the frog's path green.

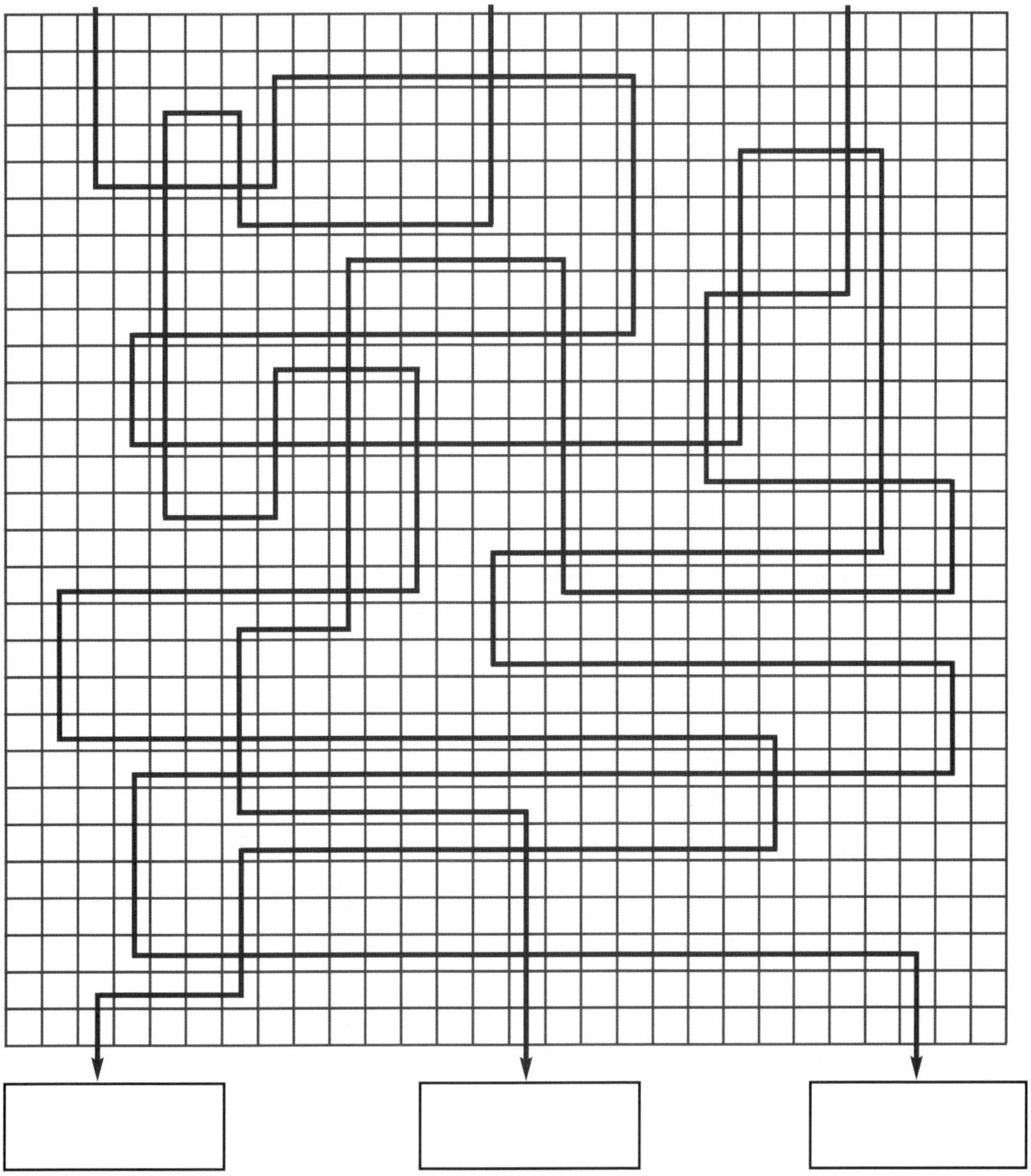

Coded Pattern (1)

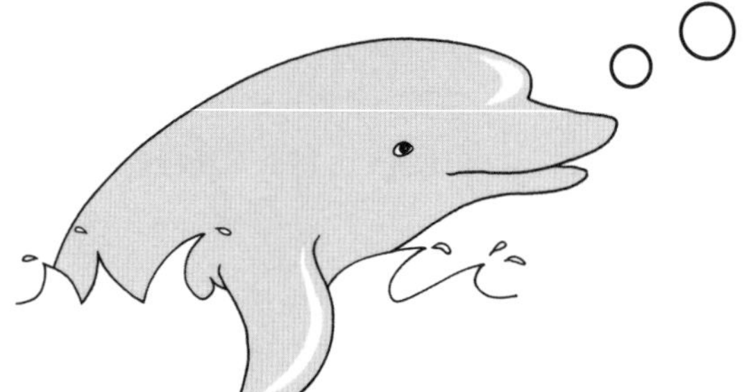

1	2	1	11	7	6	7	11	10	2	10
2	5	0	3	9	13	14	3	14	5	2
1	0	8	12	4	4	4	12	8	0	1
11	3	12	10	2	1	11	7	8	13	6
7	14	4	2	13	9	13	6	12	9	7
6	13	4	10	14	4	14	10	14	3	11
10	9	12	11	5	0	3	2	8	0	10
11	5	8	7	6	1	11	7	12	5	2
1	0	4	12	8	4	12	8	4	9	1
2	3	14	3	9	13	0	5	14	13	6
7	2	10	11	1	6	10	2	7	11	7

Colour the squares as shown below.
Squares numbered 1, 7, 10 = yellow
Squares numbered 2, 6, 11 = blue
Squares numbered 0, 9, 14 = red
Squares numbered 3, 5, 13 = green
Squares numbered 4, 8, 12 = one colour of your choice.

© Andrew Brodie Publications   www.acblack.com   WET PLAY TODAY

Coded Pattern (2)

1	2	3	4	5	6	7	8	9	10	11	12	13
14	15	16	17	18	19	20	21	22	23	24	25	26
27	28	29	30	31	32	33	34	35	36	37	38	39
40	41	42	43	44	45	46	47	48	49	50	51	52
53	54	55	56	57	58	59	60	61	62	63	64	65
66	67	68	69	70	71	72	73	74	75	76	77	78
79	80	81	82	83	84	85	86	87	88	89	90	91
92	93	94	95	96	97	98	99	100	101	102	103	104
105	106	107	108	109	110	111	112	113	114	115	116	117
118	119	120	121	122	123	124	125	126	127	128	129	130
131	132	133	134	135	136	137	138	139	140	141	142	143
144	145	146	147	148	149	150	151	152	153	154	155	156
157	158	159	160	161	162	163	164	165	166	167	168	169

Colour the squares as shown below.

Blue: 1, 13, 15, 25, 29, 37, 43, 49, 57, 61, 71, 73, 85, 97, 99, 109, 113, 121, 127, 133, 141, 145, 155, 157, 169

Red: 2, 12, 14 ,16, 24 ,26, 28 ,30, 36 ,38, 42 ,44, 48 ,50, 56 ,58, 60 ,62, 70 ,72, 74 ,84, 86 ,96, 98 ,100, 108, 110, 112, 114, 120, 122, 126, 128, 132, 134, 140, 142, 144, 146, 154, 156, 158, 168

Green: 5, 9, 19, 21, 33, 53, 65, 67, 77, 81, 89, 93, 103, 105, 117, 137, 149, 151, 161, 165

Yellow: 6, 7, 8, 20, 66, 78, 79, 80, 90, 91, 92, 104, 150, 162, 163, 164

Colour ALL the other squares using ONE other colour of your choice.

The Puzzle Wall

Follow the number code to colour
the bricks the correct colours.

Bricks marked: 0, 3, 5 = Blue
Bricks marked: 1, 9, 7 = Green
Bricks marked: 2, 8 = Yellow
Bricks marked: 4, 6 = Red

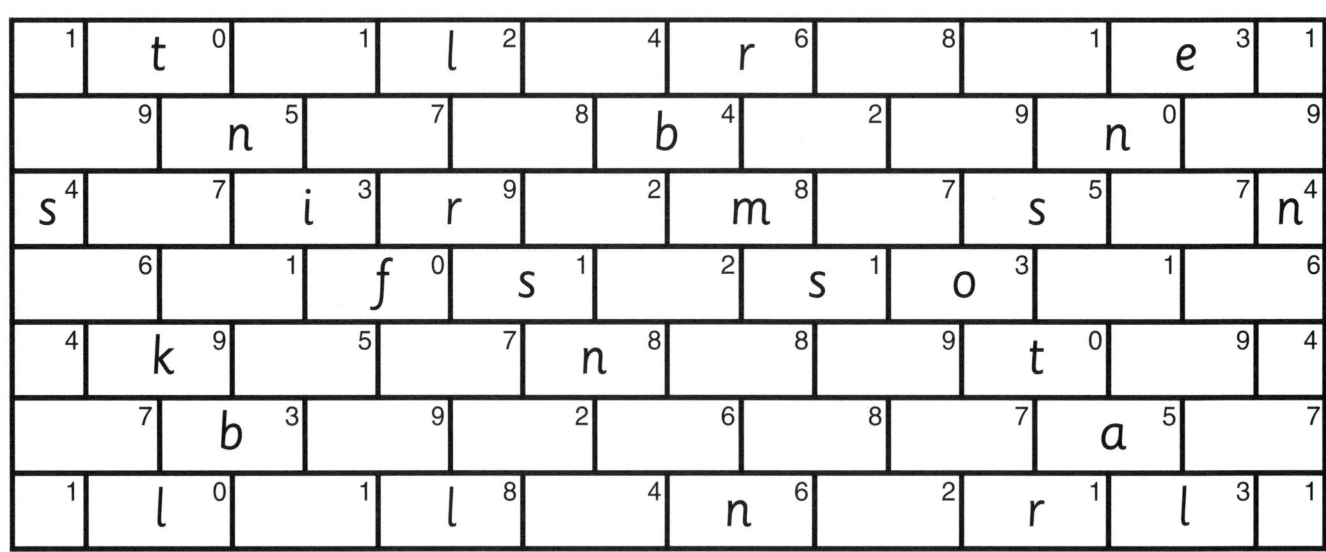

Some of the bricks have letters.
Starting from the top, read the BLUE bricks from left to
right to find Ben's favourite games.

Ben likes to play _ _ _ _ _ _ _ and _ _ _ _ _ _ _ _ _ _.

   © Andrew Brodie Publications   www.acblack.com   WET PLAY TODAY

Four Colour Puzzle (1)

- Choose only FOUR different colours.
- Use them to colour the circle puzzle below.
- No section must be the same colour as one next to it.
- You will need to take great care to manage this with just four colours.

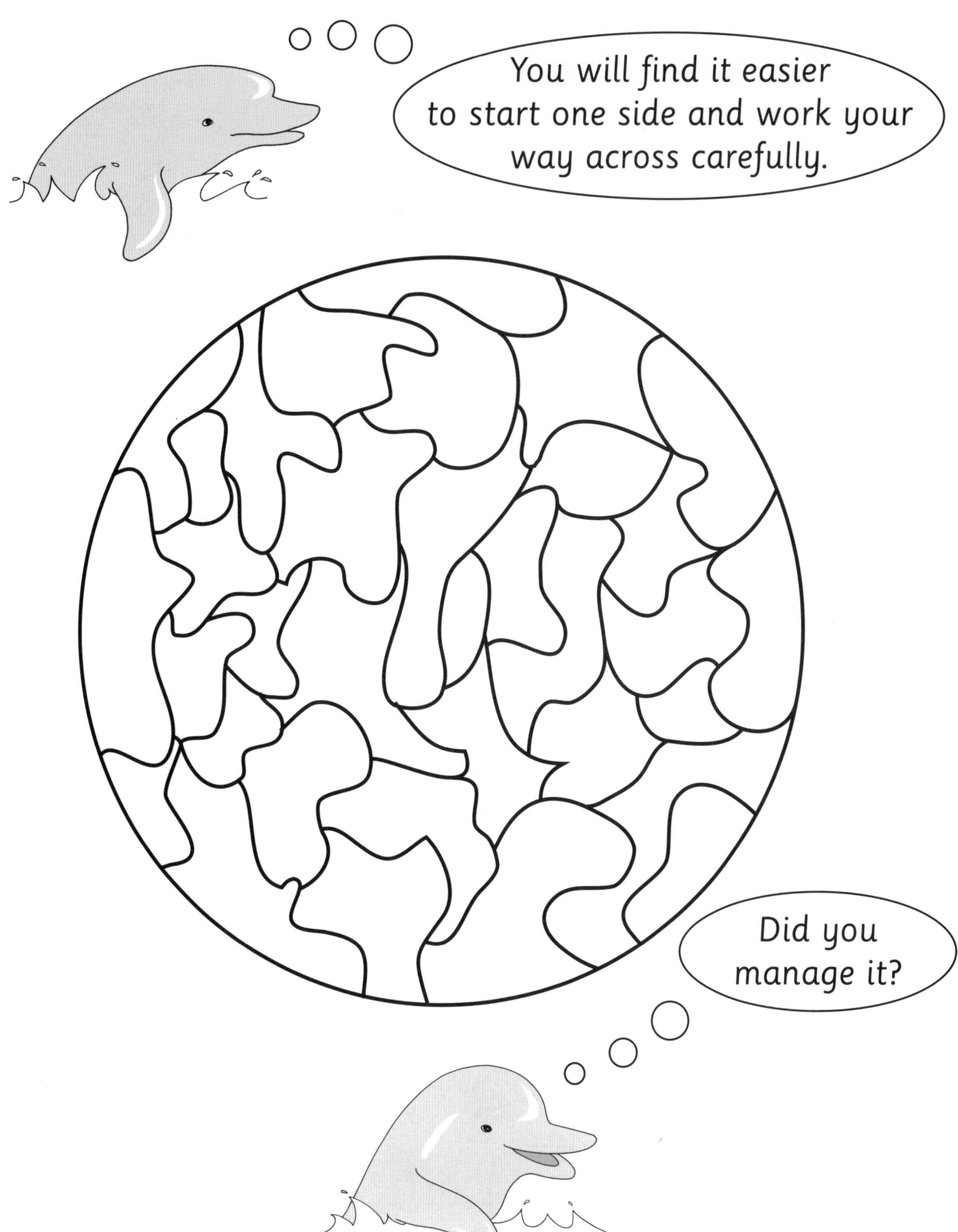

Four Colour Puzzle (2)

- Colour this puzzle using only four different colours.

- No two sections that touch one another should be the same colour.

- You will need to do this very carefully to complete the puzzle with just four colours.

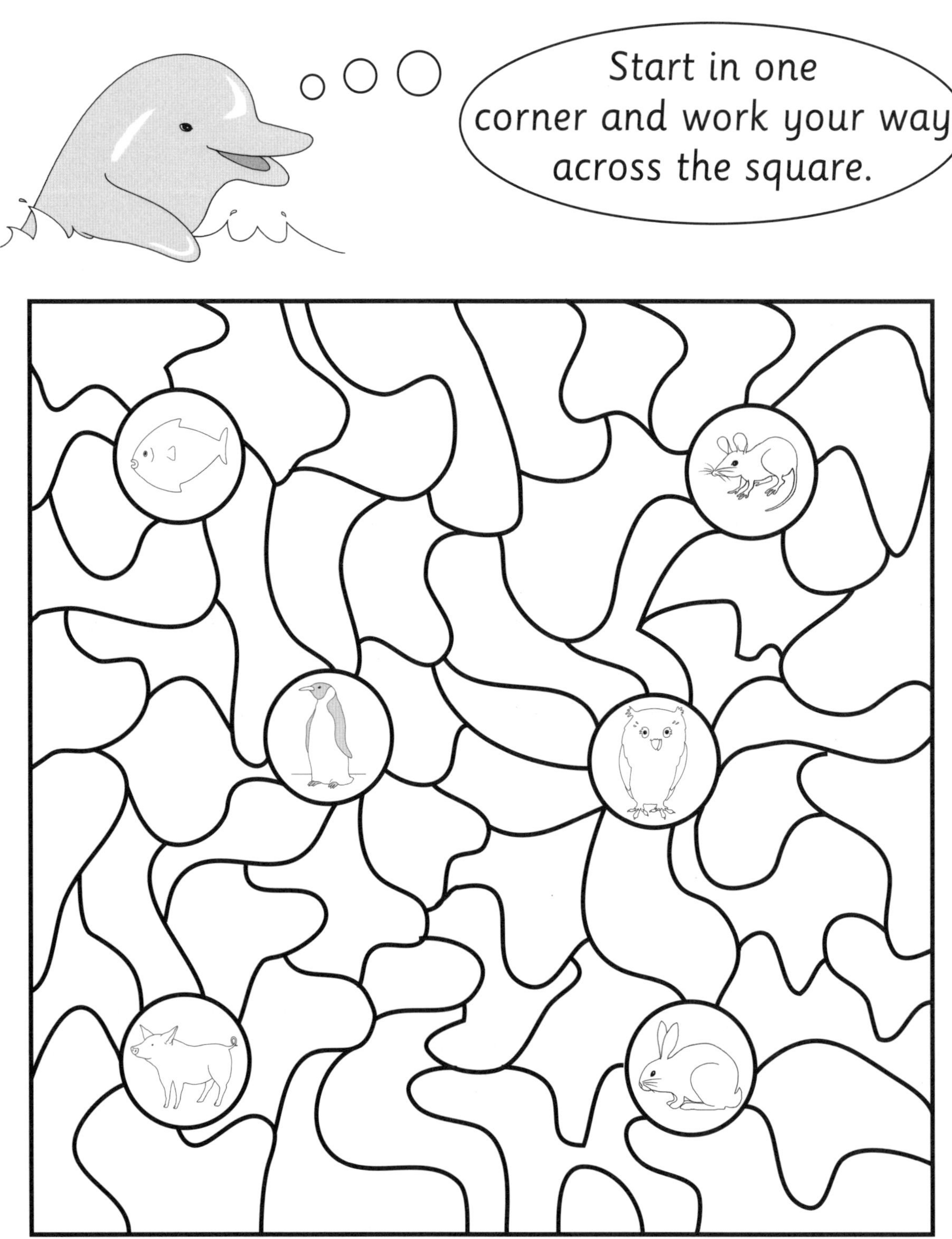

WET PLAY TODAY

Puzzle Picture

Find out what is standing in the countryside.
Follow the code to colour the squares.

A	U	V	X	U	V	W	X	B
U	B	W	Y	V	Z	Y	C	U
V	W	C	Z	U	X	D	V	W
X	Y	Z	D	V	E	X	Y	Z
U	V	W	X	C	Y	Z	Y	Z
X	V	W	E	G	D	X	W	U
U	Y	D	I	J	H	E	X	U
V	C	F	K	H	L	G	C	Y
A	Z	I	K	G	H	I	U	B
X	W	F	M	J	N	G	V	W
U	V	G	H	F	J	I	U	X
P	Q	H	G	M	H	J	R	S
S	R	I	F	O	I	G	Q	T

Letters: A, B, C, D, E = Red
F, G, H, I, J = Grey
K, L, M, N, O = Yellow
P, Q, R, S, T = Green
U, V, W, X, Y, Z = Blue

Complete the Square Pictures

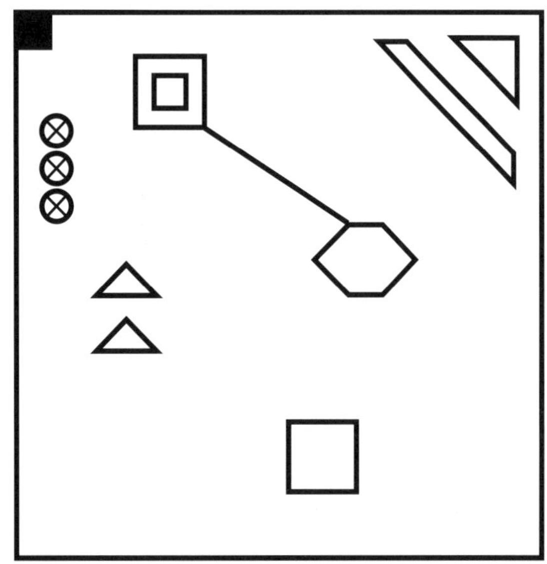

These pictures should all be the same.
Draw in the missing items needed to complete each one.
Use a ruler to draw any straight lines.

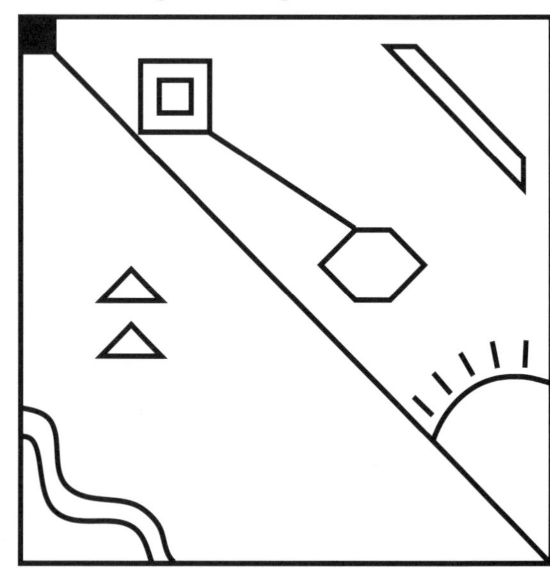

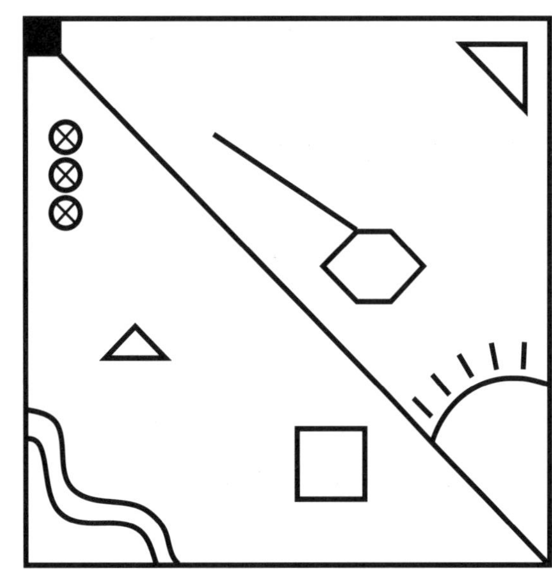

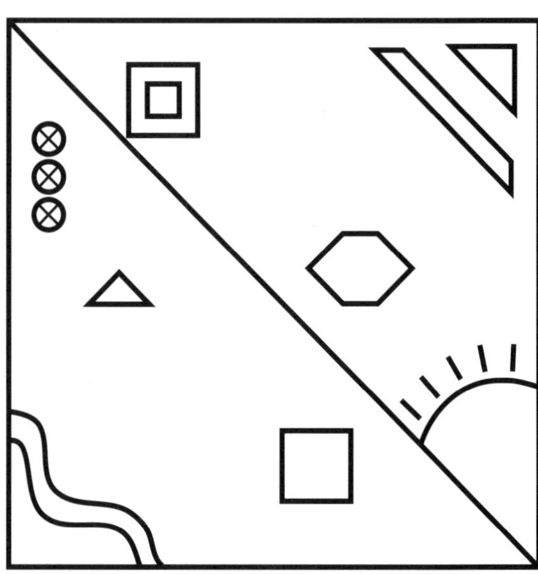

© Andrew Brodie Publications   www.acblack.com   WET PLAY TODAY

Complete the Octagon Pictures

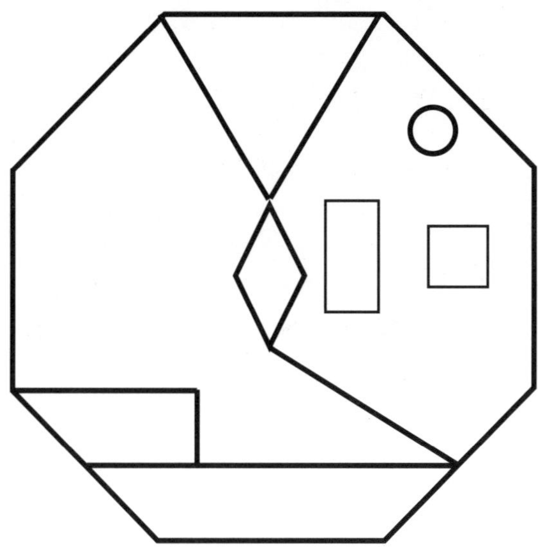 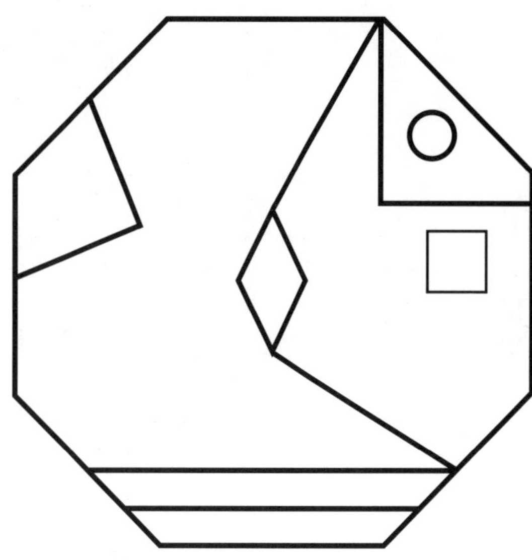

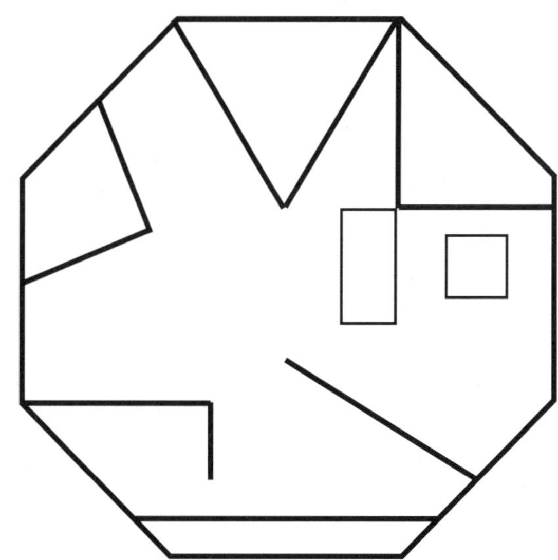 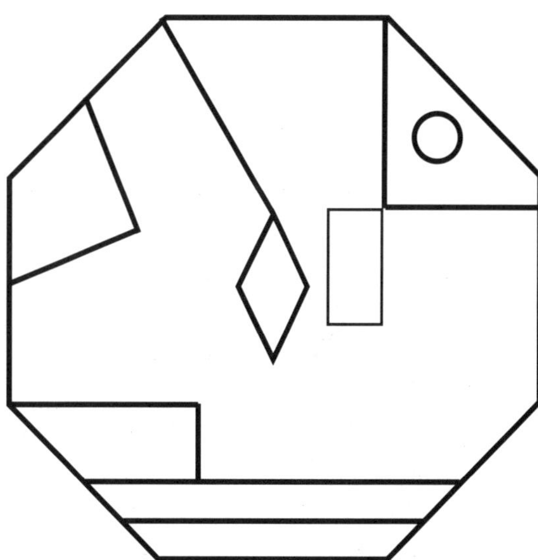

Complete the Circle Pictures

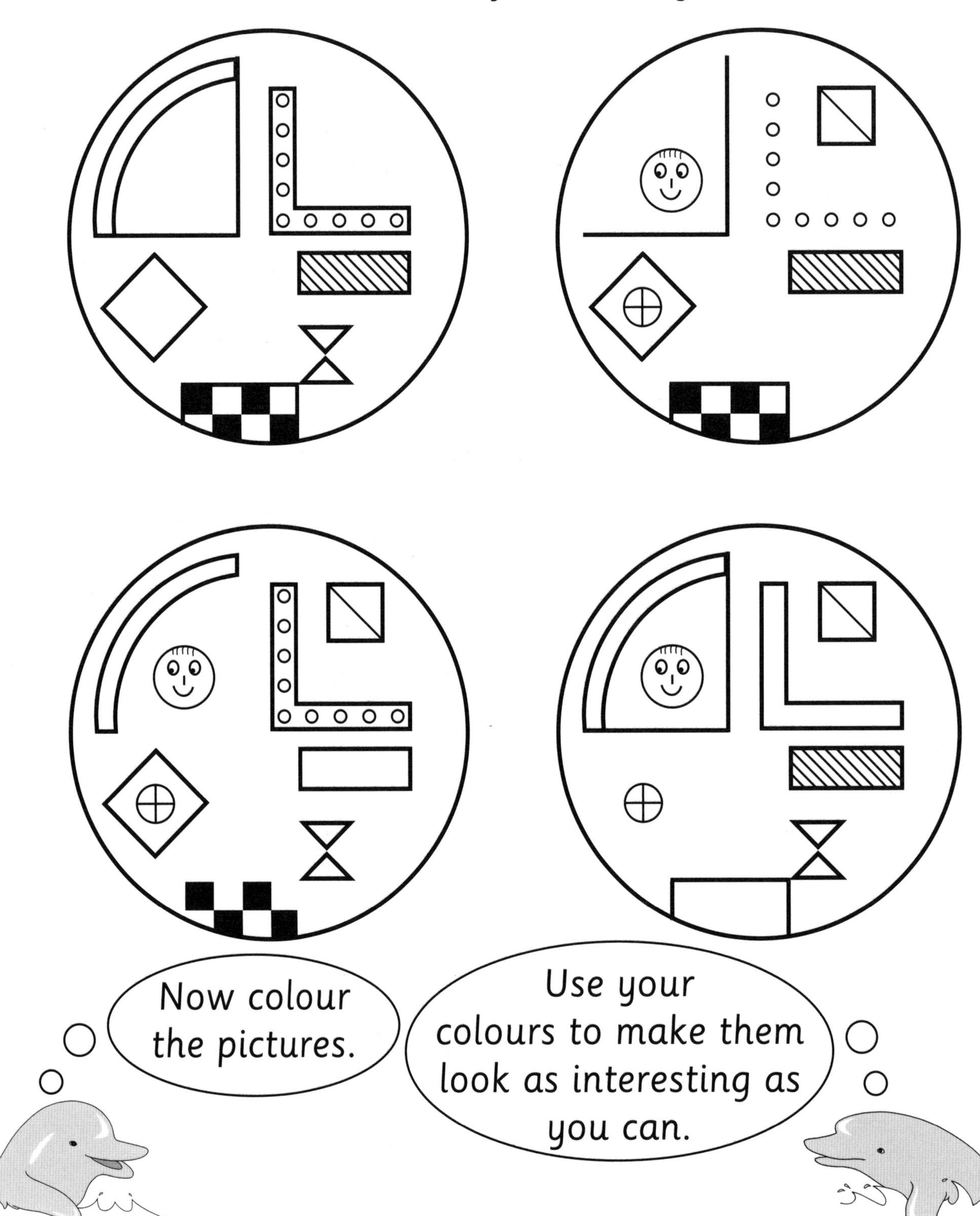

      WET PLAY TODAY

Complete the Triangle Pictures

△ These three pictures should all be the same.
△ Draw in the missing items to make them identical.
△ Use a ruler to draw the straight lines.

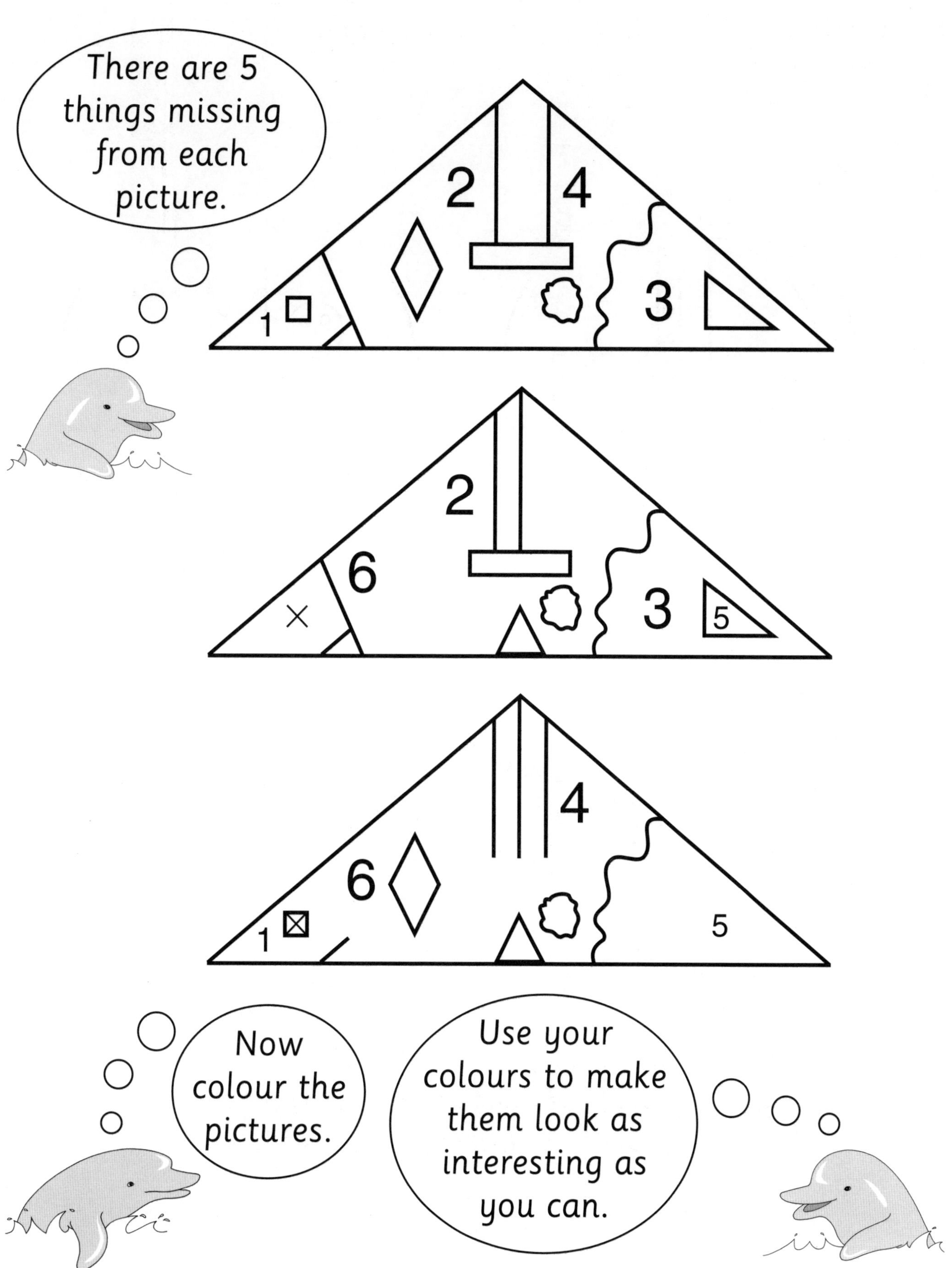

Down on the Farm

Label the pictures correctly, then find the words in the hay bale wordsearch.
The words are all written horizontally → or vertically ↓.

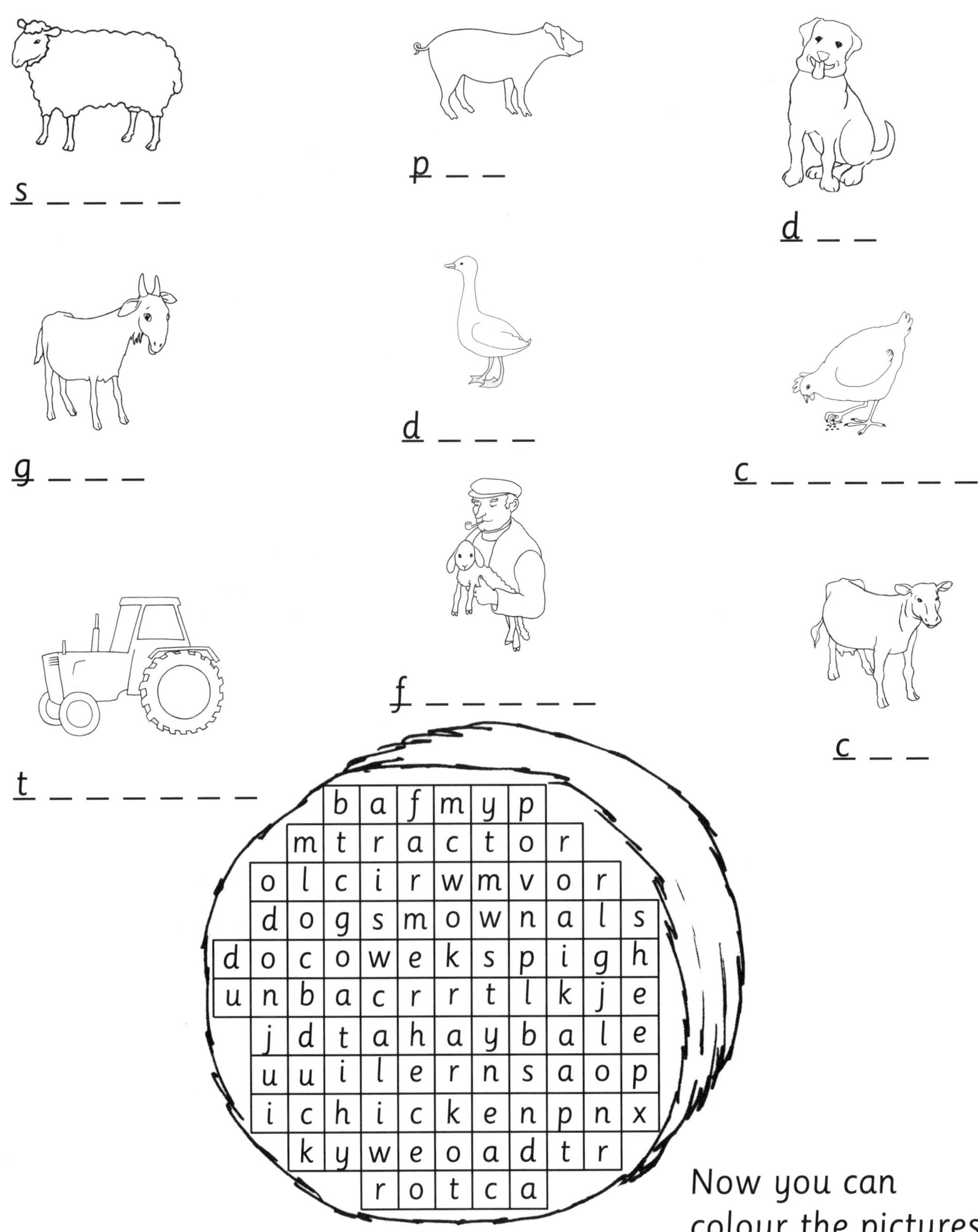

b	a	f	m	y	p		
m	t	r	a	c	t	o	r
o	l	c	i	r	w	m	v	o	r
d	o	g	s	m	o	w	n	a	l	s
d	o	c	o	w	e	k	s	p	i	g	h
u	n	b	a	c	r	r	t	l	k	j	e
j	d	t	a	h	a	y	b	a	l	e
u	u	i	l	e	r	n	s	a	o	p
i	c	h	i	c	k	e	n	p	n	x
k	y	w	e	o	a	d	t	r
r	o	t	c	a

Now you can colour the pictures.

  © Andrew Brodie Publications   www.acblack.com   WET PLAY TODAY

Animal Babies

* Below you will find the muddled names of baby animals.
* Using the picture clues to help you, write each name correctly.
* Find all the baby animals in the wordsearch.
* The wordsearch will help you to check your spellings.

ckcih

_ _ _ _ _

tyngce

_ _ _ _ _ _

ubc

_ _ _

blma

_ _ _ _

plitge

_ _ _ _ _ _

nkikte

_ _ _ _ _ _

eyoj

_ _ _ _

floa

_ _ _ _

a	j	a	m	y	d	o	l	s	w	b	c	u	b	k	c	a	b	r	c
o	l	c	g	p	u	p	p	y	d	i	y	n	n	s	y	o	c	d	a
r	c	m	i	r	a	d	g	e	m	e	l	t	i	n	g	s	i	m	l
p	h	l	e	a	j	p	i	g	l	e	t	x	e	k	n	l	u	h	f
k	i	t	t	e	n	s	h	e	p	w	e	h	o	r	e	s	d	o	e
a	c	l	a	f	m	s	e	u	o	f	o	a	l	p	t	k	i	d	w
l	k	s	d	i	j	o	e	y	r	n	b	a	o	f	d	e	i	n	w
l	u	b	r	j	a	k	o	d	e	e	n	a	p	h	a	n	t	o	w
l	t	d	u	c	k	l	i	n	g	l	a	m	b	r	a	u	c	t	o

There are 4 other baby animals in the wordsearch.
Can you find them as well?

Nursery Rhyme Code

These nursery rhyme and story titles are written in code.
Follow the code to find out what they are.
The first one has been done for you.

A	B	C	D	E	F	G	H	I	J	K	L	M
z	y	x	w	v	u	t	s	r	q	p	o	n

N	O	P	Q	R	S	T	U	V	W	X	Y	Z
m	l	k	j	i	h	g	f	e	d	c	b	a

The coded words are made using the lower case letters from
the boxes above. Write down the capital letter
which is written above it to find the answers.

1. x r m w v i v o o z

    <u>C</u> <u>I</u> <u>N</u> <u>D</u> <u>E</u> <u>R</u> <u>E</u> <u>L</u> <u>L</u> <u>A</u>

2. y v z f g b   z m w   g s v   y v z h g

    _ _ _ _ _ _   _ _ _   _ _ _   _ _ _ _

3. t l o w r o l x p h   z m w

    _ _ _ _ _ _ _ _ _ _   _ _ _

    g s v   g s i v v   y v z i h

    _ _ _   _ _ _ _ _ _   _ _ _ _

4. s r x p l i b   w r x p l i b   w l x p

    _ _ _ _ _ _ _   _ _ _ _ _ _ _   _ _ _ _

5. g s v   f t o b   w f x p o r m t

    _ _ _   _ _ _ _   _ _ _ _ _ _ _ _

6. g s i v v   y o r m w   n r x v

    _ _ _ _ _   _ _ _ _ _   _ _ _ _

Use the code to make up
some words for a friend to do.

   © Andrew Brodie Publications   www.acblack.com   WET PLAY TODAY

Jumper Code

Find out the teddy's name by following
the code to colour his jumper.

Animal Antics - Rabbit

A game for 2, 3 or 4 players.
Be the first to complete a rabbit.

You will need: 1 die marked 1 to 6
coloured pencils

How to play:

- Each player chooses a rabbit.

- Roll the die in turn.

- Colour one segment of your rabbit to match the number rolled.

- If the number is not available, miss a turn.

- The winner is the first to complete their rabbit.

   WET PLAY TODAY

Animal Antics - Elephant

A game for 2, 3 or 4 players.
Be the first to complete an elephant.

You will need: 1 die marked 1 to 6
                  coloured pencils

How to play.
- Each player chooses an elephant.
- Roll the die in turn.
- Colour one segment of your elephant to match the number rolled.
- If the number is not available, miss a turn.
- The winner is the first to complete their elephant.

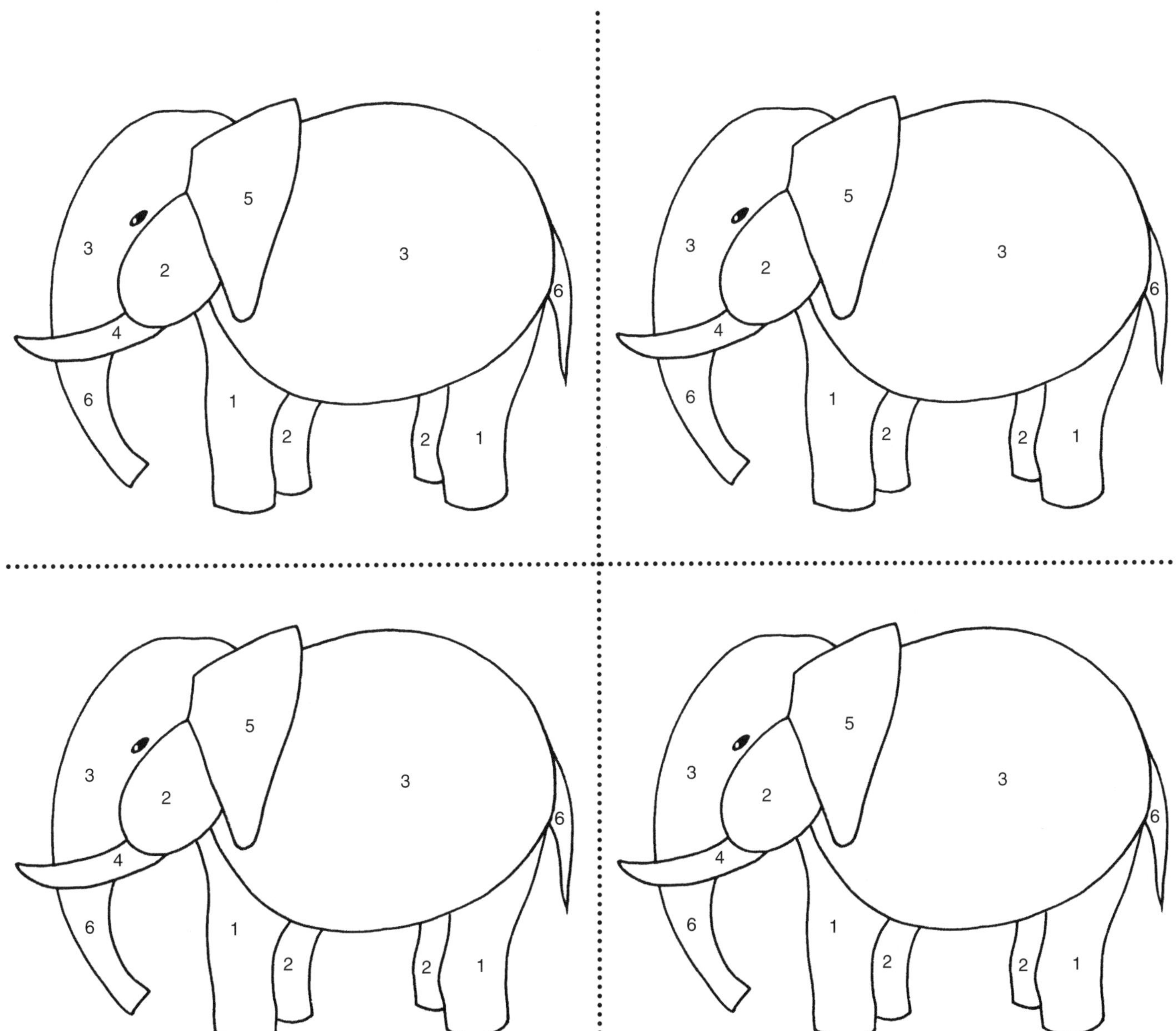

Animal Antics - Dog

A game for 2, 3 or 4 players.
Be the first to complete a dog.

You will need: 1 die marked 1 to 6
coloured pencils

How to play:

- Each player chooses a dog.

- Roll the die in turn.

- Colour one segment of your dog to match the number rolled.

- If the number is not available, miss a turn.

- The winner is the first to complete their dog.

   © Andrew Brodie Publications   www.acblack.com   WET PLAY TODAY

Animal Antics - Cat

A game for 2, 3 or 4 players.
Be the first to complete a cat.

You will need: 1 die marked 1 to 6
coloured pencils

How to play:

Each player chooses a cat.

Roll the die in turn.

Colour one segment of your cat to match the number rolled.

If the number is not available, miss a turn.

The winner is the first to complete their cat.

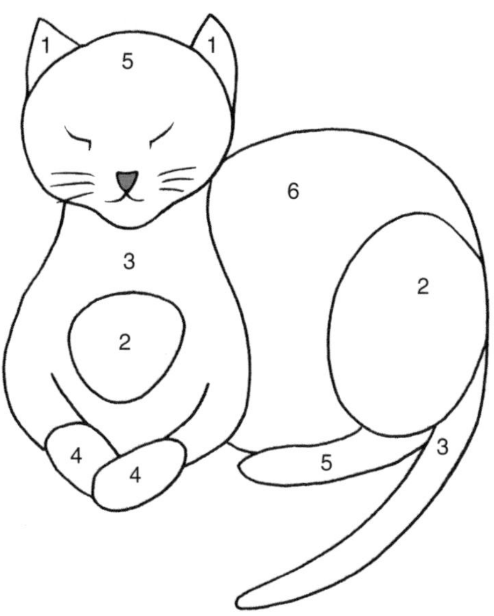

Alphabet Pictures

Match the alphabet to the pictures.
The first one is done for you.

a   b   c   d   e   f   g   h   i   j   k   l   m

n   o   p   q   r   s   t   u   v   w   x   y   z

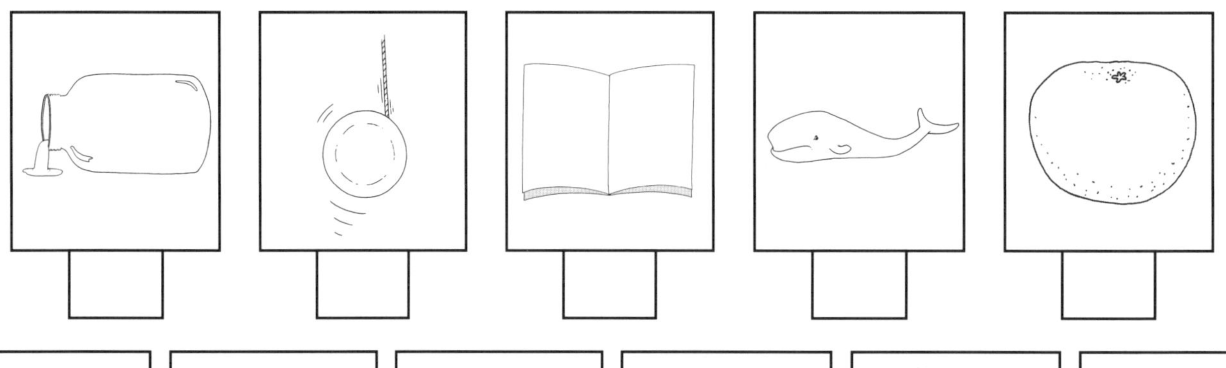

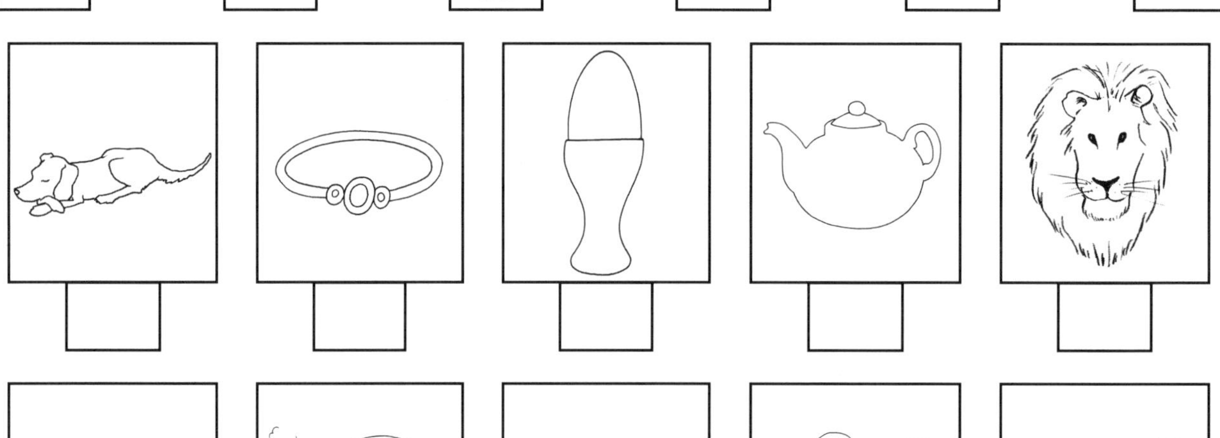

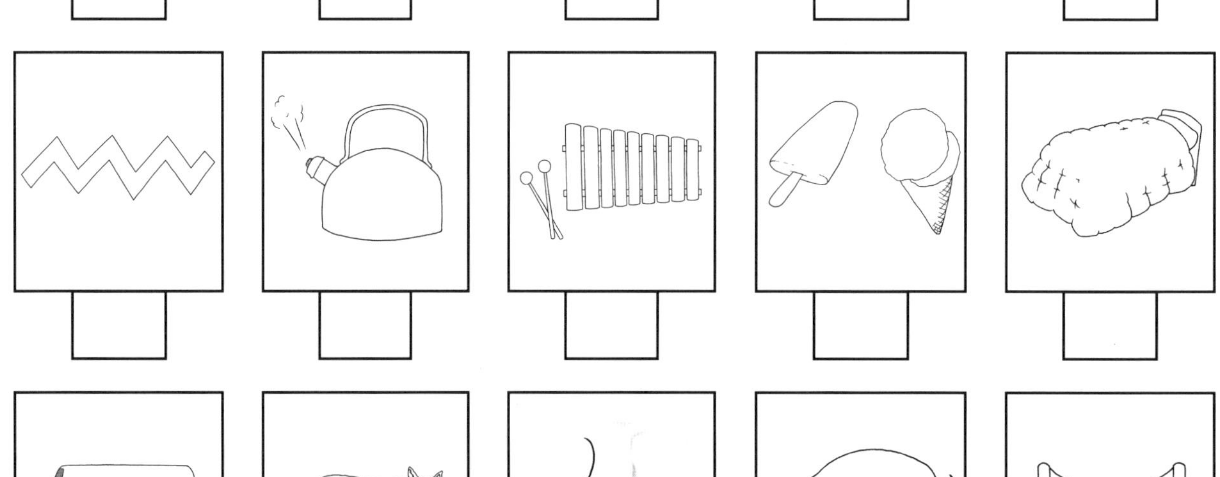

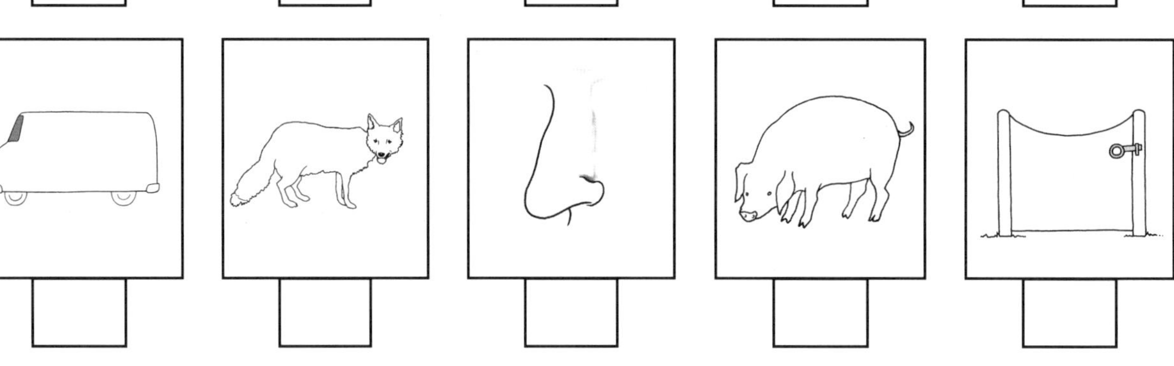

   © Andrew Brodie Publications   www.acblack.com   WET PLAY TODAY

20mm Square Grid

WET PLAY TODAY

20mm Equilateral Grid

WET PLAY TODAY